Practical English 1

TIM HARRIS

Illustrated by ALLAN ROWE

HARCOURT BRACE JOVANOVICH, INC.

NEW YORK   SAN DIEGO   CHICAGO   SAN FRANCISCO   ATLANTA

LONDON   SYDNEY   TORONTO

Preface

Practical English is a new series designed to teach English as a second or a foreign language. Students who use *Practical English* will learn all four language skills—listening, speaking, reading, and writing—from the beginning. In book 1 the emphasis is on oral communication; the later books give increased attention to reading and writing. Supplementary materials include workbooks and tape cassettes for additional writing and listening practice, and instructor's manuals containing useful teaching suggestions and answers to all text and workbook exercises.

In writing *Practical English* our overriding concern has been to create material that is appropriate for adult and secondary-school students. This has been accomplished by using a broad range of characters and real-life situations to teach the language. The grammar is presented in a way that takes advantage of the greater maturity and reasoning power of students at the adult and secondary levels. Structural items are demonstrated, rather than taught in the form of rules to be memorized. Students are encouraged to form their own conclusions based on the examples given. The idea is to get the students involved in a creative learning process that encourages them to develop their grammatical intuition.

There is no question that mature students need a sound working knowledge of grammar if they are to be confident and creative in using their new language. However, it is not enough to master the grammatical structures of English. Students must be able to relate the language to their own personal needs and interests. For this reason, *Practical English* includes a number of open-ended exercises that allow for free expression.

The free-response questions in *Practical English 1* give students the opportunity to talk about themselves using simple, straightforward English. Once they have progressed beyond the elementary level, they are ready for more creative language practice. Responding to this need, books 2 and 3 offer a wide variety of discussion topics, such as sports, hobbies, music, cinema, travel, dating, and marriage. Ideas for sketches have been provided to give additional opportunities for free expression. The general themes are familiar to students, as they are drawn from the dialogues and stories in the text.

Among the outstanding features of *Practical English* are the following:

1. **Preliminary oral work.** We feel that beginning students should have the opportunity to hear and use the target language before they open their books. Direct interaction between instructor and students makes it possible to engage in meaningful communication from the first day of class. It also helps students learn correct pronunciation and intonation. In the instructor's manual we have included detailed, easy-to-follow suggestions for introducing new structures orally, without the aid of a text. It should be emphasized that these are only suggestions of possible ways to present the basic grammar points; it is hoped that instructors will develop their own techniques for presenting these items.

2. **Illustrated situations.** As soon as a given item has been introduced orally, students should encounter it in a situational context. This ordinarily takes the form of an illustrated situation accompanied by a short reading or story. The students are asked to describe the illustration, using known grammar and vocabulary, before hearing the accompanying text. This oral activity helps students retain what they have already learned and serves as a lead-in for the text, which has been specially written to teach the

new structure. The instructor may read the text to the class or have students listen to it from a tape. Then they answer questions based on the text, while looking at the illustration. Students will find it necessary to use the new structure in responding to these questions.

3. Dialogues. Each chapter in the books is divided into three units. Units A and B generally begin with an illustrated situation featuring a basic grammatical structure. The structure appears next in a situational dialogue with pictures to help students understand the meaning of the statements. As with the illustrated situations, the dialogues may be read to the class or heard from a tape. When students have had sufficient practice in listening to a particular dialogue and repeating the statements, the instructor may ask comprehension questions based on the text. The dialogues are short and well defined, so that students can learn them quickly and act out the parts. As an alternative to acting, students may be asked to reconstruct a given dialogue by referring only to the pictures.

4. Drills. The illustrated situations and dialogues are followed by oral exercises or drills, which give further practice in using the same structures. The various exercise techniques include transformation, question-and-answer, substitution, and sentence completion. The drills are relatively simple at the beginning of each chapter, becoming more difficult toward the end. They are designed to help students acquire language concepts, as well as accuracy and fluency in speaking.

5. Reading passages. Unit C of most chapters opens with an illustrated reading passage that combines new structures with previous material in a natural context. The passage is followed by a series of comprehension questions that can be done orally or in written form, in class or at home. The reading passage provides a useful context for class conversation and, in many instances, for sketches.

By the time students come to the reading passage they will generally have sufficient confidence in using the new structures to do a sketch based on the story. Acting-out situations should be encouraged whenever possible, as this gives students a chance to be spontaneous and original in using their new language. Accordingly, the major portion of each book is given over to illustrated situations, dialogues, and reading passages, all of which promote dramatization and interaction on the part of students.

6. Review drills. In addition to the reading passage, unit C contains review drills and exercises designed to reinforce and consolidate what has been learned in units A and B. The exercises in unit C are generally more difficult than those in units A and B and may be assigned as homework.

Unit C also has lists of new vocabulary and expressions, followed by pronunciation exercises. The pronunciation exercises focus on sounds that have proved difficult for students of English as a second or a foreign language.

7. Grammar frames. At the end of unit C there are grammar frames that summarize the basic structures taught in the chapter, confirming what students have learned through concrete observation and practice. The grammar frames allow students to review at home the structural material they have been learning in class.

Students using *Practical English* will find it much easier to assimilate the basic grammar points as they encounter each item in a variety of contexts.

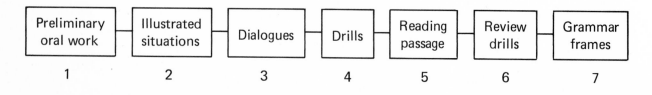

Preliminary oral work	Illustrated situations	Dialogues	Drills	Reading passage	Review drills	Grammar frames
1	2	3	4	5	6	7

Each volume of *Practical English* is accompanied by a workbook, called *Writing Practical English*. The lessons in the workbook are closely coordinated with the lessons in the text. They provide additional writing practice in using the same grammatical structures.

There is also a cassette tape accompanying each volume of the text. The tapes include the dialogues, stories, and pronunciation exercises in *Practical English*. They give students an opportunity to hear English spoken by native speakers representing all age groups.

The teaching methods used in this series will provide students with a good functional knowledge of grammar. Having each structure demonstrated in a variety of contexts enables students to make generalizations about the language that are reliable and useful. They develop a "language sense," a feeling for words that carries over into their daily use of English. As a result, they can say what they want to say and have it stay with them outside the classroom.

To our families—
and two very special Cariocas

ACKNOWLEDGMENTS

We wish to thank Ann Karat, Alisa Blatt, Tony Harris, Bennetta Hamilton, and Judy Henri
for their valuable assistance in the preparation of this series.
And special thanks to Kern Krapohl for contributing some of the best stories.

Contents

CHAPTER ONE

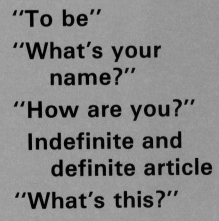

PETER: Hello. What's your name?

MARIA: My name's Maria.

PETER: My name's Peter.

MARIA: Nice to meet you, Peter.

BARBARA: Good morning.

TINO: Good morning. How are you?

BARBARA: I'm fine. And you?

TINO: Fine, thank you.

This is John Bascomb.

He's a banker.

This is Maria Miranda.

She's a doctor.

This is Peter Smith.

He's a businessman.

This is Anne Jones.

She's a secretary.

This is Nancy Paine.

She isn't a doctor.

She's a pilot.

This is Otis Jackson.

He isn't a businessman.

He's an artist.

This is Ula Hackey.

She isn't a secretary.

She's a movie star.

This is Nick Vitakis.

He isn't a banker.

He's a mechanic.

FRED: Who's that?

BARNEY: Her name is Nancy Paine.

FRED: Is she a mechanic?

BARNEY: No, she isn't.

FRED: What is she?

BARNEY: She's a pilot.

FRED: What's his name?

BARNEY: Otis Jackson.

FRED: Is he a pilot, too?

BARNEY: No, he isn't. He's
            an artist.

a 1. What's this?

It's a book.

2. What's this?

It's a chair.

3. What's this?

_____ bottle.

4. What's this?

_____ hat.

5. Is this a clock?

Yes, it is.

6. Is this a table?

Yes, it is.

7. Is this a book?
What is it?

No, it isn't.
It's a newspaper.

8. Is this a bottle?
What is it?

No, it isn't.
_____ glass.

9. Is this a clock?
What is it?

_____ .
_____ watch.

10. Is this a hat?
What is it?

_____ .
_____ coat.

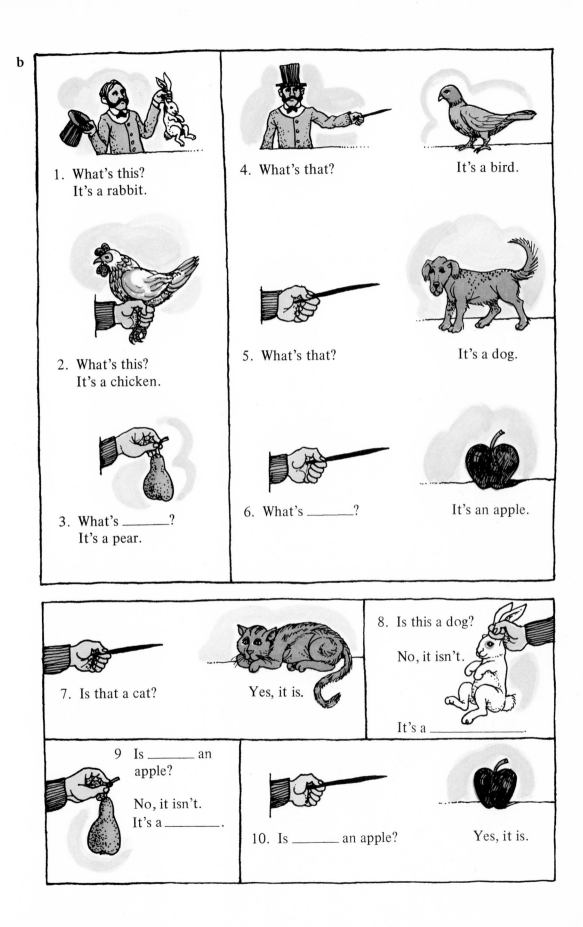

b

1. What's this?
It's a rabbit.

2. What's this?
It's a chicken.

3. What's _____?
It's a pear.

4. What's that?   It's a bird.

5. What's that?   It's a dog.

6. What's _____?   It's an apple.

7. Is that a cat?   Yes, it is.

8. Is this a dog?
No, it isn't.
It's a _____.

9 Is _____ an apple?
No, it isn't.
It's a _____.

10. Is _____ an apple?   Yes, it is.

c

1. What are these?
   They're flowers.

2. What are these?
   They're cards.

3. What are _____?
   They're rabbits.

4. What are those?

They're chickens.

5. What are those?

They're cats.

6. What are _____?

They're dogs.

7. Are these rabbits?
   Yes, they are.

8. Are those pears?

Yes, they are.

9. Are _____ cats?

No, they aren't.
They're _____.

10. Are _____ apples?

No, they aren't.
They're _____.

The cat is <u>under</u> the table.

    The ball is <u>in front of</u> the cat.

The vase is <u>on</u> the table.

    The flower is <u>in</u> the vase.

The envelope is <u>on</u> the table.

    The envelope is <u>next to</u> the vase.

The bookcase is <u>behind</u> the table.

    The books are <u>in</u> the bookcase.

d   1. Where's the cat now?
        It's _____ the table.

     2. Where's the dog?
        It's _____ the table.

     3. Where's the vase?
        It's _____ the floor.

     4. Where's the flower?
        It's _____ the vase.

     5. Where's the envelope?
        It's _____ the cat.

     6. Where's the ball?
        It's _____ the dog.

1

Ula Hackey is at the movies.

2

Otis is at the museum.

3

Mr. Bascomb is at the bank.

4

Nick is at the garage.

5

Maria is at the hospital.

6

Peter is at the office.

7

Nancy is at the airport.

8

Anne is at the post office.

9

Barney is at the gas station.

a   *Replace with **he** or **she**.*

1. Ula is at the movies.
   She's at the movies.
2. Otis is at the museum.
   He's at the museum.
3. Mr. Bascomb is at the bank.
4. Nick is at the garage.

5. Maria is at the hospital.
6. Peter is at the office.
7. Nancy is at the airport.
8. Anne is at the post office.
9. Barney is at the gas station.

b   *Look at the pictures on page 10 and answer the following questions.*

1. Is Ula at the movies?
   Yes, she is.
2. Is Otis at the post office?
   No, he isn't. He's at the museum.
3. Is Mr. Bascomb at the hospital?
4. Is Nick at the garage?

5. Is Maria at the airport?
6. Is Peter at the office?
7. Is Nancy at the movies?
8. Is Anne at the bank?
9. Is Barney at the gas station?

c   *Change the following sentences to the interrogative.*

Example: He is a banker.
         Is he a banker?

1. She is a pilot.
2. He is a taxi driver.
3. She is a doctor.
4. He is an artist.

5. He is a mechanic.
6. She is a secretary.
7. He is a businessman.
8. She is a movie star.

d   *Complete with **a** or **an**.*

Examples: It's _____ glass.   It's _____ egg.
           It's <u>a</u> glass.   **It's <u>an</u> egg.**

1. It's _____ tree.
2. It's _____ apple.
3. It's _____ car.

4. It's _____ bottle.
5. It's _____ orange.
6. It's _____ envelope.

7. It's _____ library.
8. It's _____ newspaper.
9. It's _____ airport.

a car

a library

a tree

an apple

an orange

an egg

Note: *a* before consonant   *an* before a, e, i, o, u

e *Complete the sentences.*

Example: Where's the bus stop? It's _____*at*_____ the corner.

1. Where's Barbara? She's _____ the bus stop.

2. Where's the truck? It's _____ the bus.

3. Where's the post office? It's _____ the garage.

4. Where's the tree? It's _____ the garage.

5. Where's the car? It's _____ the garage.

6. Where's Nick? He's _____ the car.

f *Answer the following questions about the picture.*

Examples: Is the bus stop at the corner?
Yes, it is.

Is Barbara in the post office?
No, she isn't. She's at the bus stop.

1. Is the truck behind the bus?
2. Is the post office next to the garage?
3. Is the tree behind the post office?
4. Is the car in front of the garage?
5. Is Nick in the car?

g   *Complete the sentences as indicated.*

1. What's _*this*_? It's _*a hat*_.

2. What's _____? It's _____.

3. What's _____? It's _____.

4. What's _____? It's _____.

5. What are _____? They're _____.

6. What are _____? They're _____.

7. What are _____? They're _____.

8. What are _____? They're _____.

VOCABULARY

a	businessman	garage	mechanic	pilot	truck
airplane	bus stop	gas station	meet	post office	
airport		glass	movies		under
am	car	good morning	movie star	rabbit	
an	card		Mr.		vase
and	cat	hat	museum	secretary	
apple	chair	he	my	she	watch (n.)
are	chicken	hello			what
artist	clock	her	name (n.)	table	where
at	coat	his	newspaper	taxi driver	who
	corner	hospital	next to	thank you	
ball		how	nice	that	yes
bank	doctor		no	the	you
banker	dog	I	not	these	your
behind		in		they	
bird	egg	in front of	office	this	
book	envelope	is	on	those	
bookcase		it	orange	to	
bottle	fine			too	
bus	flower	library	pear	tree	

EXPRESSIONS

Hello. What's your name?   How are you?   Where's Barbara?

My name is Maria.   I'm fine, and you?   at the corner

Nice to meet you.   Fine, thank you.   at the movies

airplane

PRONOUNCE THESE WORDS CLEARLY

ey		æ	
name	bookcase	cat	apple
vase	airplane	hat	taxi
table	newspaper	that	rabbit
station		glass	mechanic

TO BE Affirmative

He She It	's (is)	in the office.

Negative

He She It	isn't (is not) 's not	in the office.

Interrogative

Is	he she it	in the office?

Short Answers

Yes,	he she it	is.

No,	he she it	isn't.

Question with WHAT

What	's (is)	this? that?
	are	these? those?

SINGULAR AND PLURAL NOUNS

It	's (is)	a pear an apple.
They	're (are)	cards. flowers.

Question with WHERE

Where	's (is)	Mr. Bascomb?
	's (is)	the newspaper?
	are	the books?

PREPOSITIONS

He	's (is)	at in	the bank. his office.
It	's (is)	on under next to	the table.
They	're (are)	behind in front of	

Question with WHO

Who	's (is)	that?

Otis Jackson.

CHAPTER TWO

"To be" with adjective

"To be" with adjective and noun

Singular and plural nouns

Numbers 1–20

Time

WAITER: Excuse me. Are you a tourist?

TOURIST: Yes, I am.

WAITER: Are you English?

TOURIST: No, I'm not.

WAITER: What nationality are you?

TOURIST: I'm American.

a *Answer the following questions about yourself.*

Example: Are you a businessman?
        Yes, I am. OR **No, I'm not.**

1. Are you Italian?
2. Are you an artist?
3. Are you rich?
4. Are you married?
5. Are you a tourist?
6. Are you hot?
7. Are you thirsty?
8. Are you happy?
9. Are you sad?
10. Are you cold?

happy   sad

PEDRO: Are you from the United States?

STEVE: Yes, we are. We're from Hollywood.

PEDRO: Are you movie stars?

STEVE: No, we aren't movie stars. We're students.

JUANITA: Who are they?

PEDRO: They're Americans. They're
         from Hollywood.

JUANITA: Are they movie stars?

PEDRO: No, they aren't. They're students.

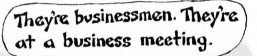

b   *Replace with* ***you, we,*** *or* ***they.***

Example: <u>Barney and I</u> are friends.
        We're friends.

1. <u>Anne and Nancy</u> are Americans.
2. <u>You and Nancy</u> are from New York.
3. <u>Anne and Peter</u> are from Los Angeles.
4. <u>Anne and I</u> are friends.
5. <u>You and Nancy</u> are friends.
6. <u>You and I</u> are students.
7. <u>Those girls </u> are students.

c   *Change the following sentences
to the interrogative.*

Example: They're businessmen.
        Are they businessmen?

1. They're at a business meeting.
2. They're at the City Bank.
3. They're on Franklin Avenue.
4. We're on Main Street.
5. We're at the post office.
6. You're doctors.
7. You're from the hospital.

d   *Change the following sentences
to the negative.*

Example: You're movie stars.
        You aren't movie stars.

1. You're tourists.
2. You're from England.
3. You're rich.
4. We're happy.
5. We're businessmen.
6. They're pilots.
7. They're Americans.

e   Tino is a waiter. He's tall and handsome. He isn't rich, but he's happy. Barbara is a secretary. She's short and blond. And she's beautiful. Barbara and Tino are good friends. They're from California.

1. Is Tino a businessman?
2. Is he short?
3. Is he handsome?
4. Is he rich?
5. Is Barbara a secretary?
6. Is she tall?
7. Is she blond?
8. Is she beautiful?
9. Are Barbara and Tino good friends?
10. Are they from New York?

f   Natalya and Boris are Russian ballet dancers. They're from Moscow. They're very good dancers.

1. Are Natalya and Boris ballet dancers or movie stars?
2. Where are they from?
3. Are they good dancers?

g   Sammy and Tammy are country singers. They're from Texas. They aren't very good singers. In fact, they're very bad.

1. Are Sammy and Tammy singers or dancers?
2. Where are they from?
3. Are they good singers?

This woman is fat.

That man is thin.

This bicycle is cheap.

That bicycle is expensive.

These women are young.

Those men are old.

These boys are dirty.

Those girls are clean.

a   *Complete the sentences about the pictures above, using these adjectives:*
bad, clean, beautiful, hot, cheap, fat, rich, married, short.

1. Barbara *is beautiful* .

2. Mr. and Mrs. Bascomb _____ .

3. Mr. Twaddle _____ .

4. Mrs. Brown _____ .

5. Albert _____ .

6. Tino _____ .

7. The pots _____ .

8. The guitar _____ .

9. The apples _____ .

b   *Answer the following questions as indicated.*

1. Is Barbara beautiful?
   Yes, she is.
2. Are Mr. and Mrs. Bascomb poor?
   No, they aren't. They're rich.
3. Is Mr. Twaddle tall?
4. Is Mrs. Brown married?
5. Is Albert thin?
6. Is Tino cold?
7. Are the pots clean?
8. Is the guitar expensive?
9. Are the apples good?

TINO: That's a beautiful red dress, Barbara.

BARBARA: Thank you, Tino. It's new.

TINO: Red is a good color for you.

BARBARA: Yes. It's my favorite color.

TINO: Are those new shoes?

BARBARA: Yes, they are. They're brand-new.

c *Change the following sentences as indicated.*

Examples: That's a pretty dress.   This is a cheap hat.
           That dress is pretty.   **This hat is cheap.**

1. That's an old newspaper.   6. This is a bad apple.
2. This is a good book.   7. That's a beautiful tree.
3. That's an expensive coat.   8. That's a clean car.
4. This is a dirty glass.   9. This is a new bicycle.
5. That's an old chair.

d *Change the above sentences from singular to plural.*

Examples: That's a pretty dress.   This is a cheap hat.
           Those are pretty dresses.   **These are cheap hats.**

NUMBERS

e   What time is it?

A.

It's one o'clock.

B.

It's eight o'clock.

C.

It's three o'clock.

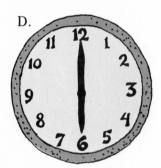
D.

E.

F.

G.

H.

I.

J.

K.

L.

Albert is with Mr. Watkins, his favorite teacher at the university.

ALBERT: Who's that girl by the window?

MR. WATKINS: It's Lúcia Mendes.

ALBERT: She's very pretty. Is she a student?

MR. WATKINS: Yes. She's a history student.

ALBERT: Is Lúcia Mexican?

MR. WATKINS: No, she isn't. She's Brazilian.

ALBERT: What city is she from?

MR. WATKINS: She's from Rio de Janeiro.

ALBERT: Is that the capital of Brazil?

MR. WATKINS: No. Brasília is the capital.

ALBERT: What's Brasília like?

MR. WATKINS: It's a beautiful modern city.

a *Answer the following questions about the dialogue.*

1. Who's Albert with?
2. Who's the girl by the window?
3. Is she very pretty?
4. Is she American?
5. What nationality is she?
6. What city is she from?
7. Is Rio de Janeiro the capital of Brazil?
8. What is the capital of Brazil?
9. What's Brasília like?

b *Complete the sentences with the correct form of the verb **to be**.*

1. Peter _____ at the office.
2. He _____ a young businessman.
3. Linda and I _____ at the university.
4. We _____ in the library.
5. It _____ a modern building.
6. Linda _____ next to the window.
7. She _____ a tall, thin girl.
8. It _____ very hot today.
9. I _____ thirsty.

Maria is at home. She's in the living room.

Mr. Bascomb is at work. He's in his office.

The children are at school. They're in the classroom.

c *Make questions as indicated.*

Examples: Maria is at home. ___*Is she*___ in the living room?

The students are at the university. ___*Are they*___ in the library?

1. Mr. Bascomb is at work. _____ in his office?

2. The children are at school. _____ in the classroom?

3. Barbara is on Maple Street. _____ at the bus stop?

4. Otis is at the museum. _____ with his friends?

5. The tourists are at the airport. _____ in the airplane?

6. Albert is at the university. _____ with Mr. Watkins?

7. Lúcia is in the classroom. _____ by the window?

8. The magazines are in the office. _____ on the desk?

9. The newspaper is in the living room. _____ on the table?

d *Answer the following questions as indicated.*

Example: Is Mr. Bascomb poor?   (rich)
No, he isn't. He's rich.

1. Is he stupid?   (intelligent)
2. Is he sad?   (happy)
3. Are Barbara and Tino married?   (single)
4. Are they old?   (young)
5. Is your car big?   (small)
6. Is it expensive?   (cheap)
7. Is it clean?   (dirty)
8. Is Albert thin?   (fat)
9. Is Sophia Loren French?   (Italian)

e *Change the following sentences as indicated.*

Examples: She's an Italian movie star.   (beautiful)
She's a beautiful Italian movie star.

They're German girls.   (young)
They're young German girls.

1. He's a young doctor.   (fine)
2. It's a red dress.   (expensive)
3. We're art students.   (young)
4. She's a ballet dancer.   (good)
5. They're school books.   (old)
6. It's an English car.   (new)
7. He's an American tourist.   (rich)
8. They're office buildings.   (modern)
9. It's a black umbrella.   (small)

an umbrella

f *Change the following sentences from singular to plural.*

Examples: It's a new dress.   She's a young woman   It's an old city.
          They're new dresses.   **They're young women.**   **They're old cities.**

1. It's an expensive car.
2. He's an old man.
3. She's an intelligent girl.
4. It's a modern building.
5. She's a good secretary.
6. He's a fine mechanic.
7. It's a new bus.
8. He's a young pilot.
9. She's a married woman.

g *Complete the sentences.*

Example: Where's the book? It's _____*on*_____ the desk.

1. Where's the teacher? He's _____ the desk.

2. Where's the wastebasket? It's _____ the desk.

3. Where's the newspaper? It's _____ the wastebasket.

4. Where's the chair? It's _____ the desk.

5. Where's the hat? It's _____ the chair.

6. Where's the umbrella? It's _____ the chair.

h *Answer the questions about the picture.*

Examples: Is the book on the desk?   Is the teacher in front of the desk?
        Yes, it is.   **No, he isn't. He's behind the desk.**

1. Is the wastebasket on the desk?
2. Is the newspaper in the wastebasket?
3. Is the chair behind the desk?
4. Is the hat on the floor?
5. Is the umbrella under the chair?

VOCABULARY

American	country singer	friend	married	sad	tourist
	cowboy	from	me	school	twelve
bad			meeting	seven	twenty
ballet	dancer	German	Mexican	seventeen	two
beautiful	desk	girl	modern	shoe	
bicycle	dirty	good	Mrs.	short	ugly
big	dress	guitar		singer	umbrella
black			nationality	single	university
blond	eight	handsome	new	six	
boy	eighteen	happy	nine	sixteen	very
brand-new	eleven	history	nineteen	small	
Brazilian	English	home		Spanish	waiter
building	excuse (v.)	hot	o'clock	student	wastebasket
business	expensive	hungry	old	stupid	we
			one		window
capital	fat	intelligent		tall	woman
cheap	favorite	Italian	poor	teacher	work
city	fifteen		pot	ten	
classroom	five	like	pretty	thin	young
clean (adj.)	floor	living room		thirsty	
cold	four		red	thirteen	
color	fourteen	magazine	rich	three	
country	French	man	Russian	time	

EXPRESSIONS

Excuse me.	What's it like?	at home	at school
What time is it?	brand-new	at work	

```
                              OPPOSITES

  hot ≠ cold        big ≠ small       good ≠ bad        beautiful ≠ ugly

  fat ≠ thin        old ≠ young       happy ≠ sad       intelligent ≠ stupid

  short ≠ tall      old ≠ new         rich ≠ poor       expensive ≠ cheap
```

PRONOUNCE THESE WORDS CLEARLY

	ay			**i**
time	pilot		this	city
like	library		big	window
fine	bicycle		rich	single
nice	behind		thin	chicken

STRESS AND INTONATION

Excuse me. Are you a tourist?

Yes, I am.

Are you English?

No, I'm not.

What nationality are you?

I'm American.

Is John a doctor?

No, he isn't. He's a banker.

What city is he from?

He's from Wickam City.

Is your name Barney or Fred?

My name is Barney.

TO BE   Affirmative

He She It	's (is)	
I	'm (am)	in the library.
You We They	're (are)	

Negative

He She It	isn't (is not) 's not	
I	'm not (am not)	in the library.
You We They	aren't (are not) 're not	

Interrogative

Is	he she it	
Am	I	in the library?
Are	you we they	

Short answers

Yes,	he she it	is.
	I	am.
	you we they	are.

No,	he she it	isn't.
	I	'm not.
	you we they	aren't.

ADJECTIVES AND WORD ORDER

The city	is	beautiful.
The buildings	are	modern.

It's	a beautiful city.
They're	modern buildings.

It's a beautiful modern city.

They're beautiful modern buildings.

PLURALS

bus	buses	city	cities
watch	watches	library	libraries
glass	glasses	secretary	secretaries

Irregular

man	men
woman	women
child	children

TIME

What time is it?

It's five o'clock.

NUMBERS 1–20

1 one	6 six	11 eleven	16 sixteen
2 two	7 seven	12 twelve	17 seventeen
3 three	8 eight	13 thirteen	18 eighteen
4 four	9 nine	14 fourteen	19 nineteen
5 five	10 ten	15 fifteen	20 twenty

PREPOSITIONS

Albert is	with	his favorite teacher.
Lúcia is	from	Rio de Janeiro.
She's	by	the window.

CHAPTER THREE

Close your book.

Stand up.

Go to the blackboard.

Write your name.

Sit down.

Be quiet.

Don't talk.

Don't write on the table.

Don't open the window.

Don't eat in class.

Don't leave the room.

Don't laugh.

Hello, Johnnie. Come with <u>me</u>.

Oh, this bottle! Please open <u>it</u>.

There's Barbara and Tino.
Let's talk with <u>them</u>.

Peter is a very good dancer. Look at <u>him</u>.

Come and sit with <u>us</u>, Peter.

There's Alice. Go and talk with <u>her</u>.

OBJECT
PRONOUNS

Look at <u>Peter</u>.	Look at <u>him</u>.
Look at <u>Maria</u>.	Look at <u>her</u>.
Look at <u>Barbara and Tino</u>.	Look at <u>them</u>.
Look at <u>Johnnie and me</u>.	Look at <u>us</u>.
Look at <u>the clock</u>.	Look at <u>it</u>.

a   *Make commands as indicated.*

Example: <u>Peter</u> is a very good dancer.
   Look at <u>him</u>.

1. <u>Barbara</u> is beautiful tonight.
2. <u>Albert</u> is very happy.
3. <u>The cat</u> is hungry.
4. <u>Those girls</u> are very tall.
5. <u>Tino and I</u> are good dancers.
6. <u>Alice</u> is a bad dancer.
7. <u>Johnnie</u> is sad.
8. <u>That clock</u> is old.
9. <u>These flowers</u> are very pretty.

b   *Change the following sentences as indicated.*

Example: Sit with <u>Johnnie and me</u>.   *Sit with us.*

1. Close <u>the door.</u>

2. Open <u>the windows.</u>

3. Talk to <u>Mr. Bascomb</u>.

4. Listen to <u>Barbara and me</u>.

5. Repeat <u>the question.</u>

6. Sit with <u>Alice.</u>

7. Dance with <u>Peter.</u>

8. Eat <u>those pears.</u>

9. Listen to <u>Maria.</u>

Mrs. Brown is a housewife. She's in the kitchen with her children, Jimmy and Linda.

c   *Ask and answer questions about the objects in the picture.*

Examples: cards   pots
         Where are the cards?   **Where are the pots?**
         They're on the floor.   **They're on the wall.**

1. cups   4. flowers   7. glasses
2. pots   5. magazines   8. oranges
3. books   6. candles   9. dishes

MR. BASCOMB: Good morning, Barbara.

BARBARA: Good morning, Mr. Bascomb. Here's a message from Mr. Smith.

MR. BASCOMB: Ah, yes. Please call him. Tell him the meeting is at ten o'clock.

BARBARA: Yes, Mr. Bascomb.

MR. BASCOMB: And bring me a sandwich, please. I'm hungry.

BARBARA: Yes, sir.

Call <u>Mr. Smith</u>.	Call <u>him</u>.
Ask <u>Mrs. Golo</u>.	Ask <u>her</u>.
Answer <u>the students</u>.	Answer <u>them</u>.
Call <u>Barbara and me</u>.	Call <u>us</u>.
Open <u>the window</u>.	Open <u>it</u>.

a *Complete the following sentences.*

Example: Mr. Bascomb is hungry. Bring *him* a sandwich.

1. Anne is in the hospital. Take _____ these flowers.

2. Mr. and Mrs. Golo are in France. Write _____ a letter.

3. We're thirsty. Bring _____ a bottle of Coca-Cola.

4. Jimmy is in class. Take _____ this message.

5. Mrs. Brown is here. Give _____ those magazines.

6. The children are hungry. Bring _____ the large red apples.

7. Albert is here. Give _____ your telephone number.

8. Barbara is at home. Take _____ this book.

9. We're in the kitchen. Bring _____ the glasses.

b *Make negative commands.*

Example: Bring us the glasses.
Don't bring us the glasses.

1. Give them the newspaper.
2. Take her the magazines.
3. Write me a letter.
4. Give him a postcard.
5. Bring us the dictionary.
6. Take him a book.
7. Give her the envelopes.
8. Bring me the bottle.
9. Tell them the answer.

a letter

a dictionary   a postcard

twenty-one

twenty-two

twenty-three

twenty-four

twenty-five

twenty-six

twenty-seven

twenty-eight

twenty-nine

thirty

thirty-one

thirty-two

forty

forty-one

fifty

sixty

seventy

eighty

ninety

one hundred

MR. BASCOMB: How old is that lamp?

SALESMAN: It's ninety-eight years old.

MR. BASCOMB: How much is it?

SALESMAN: It's one hundred and
                 twenty-five dollars.

MR. BASCOMB: That's a good price. Here you are,
                 young man.

SALESMAN: Thank you, sir. Have a nice day.

c   *Answer the following questions as indicated.*

Examples: How old is the lamp?
          It's ninety-eight years old.

          How much is it?
          **It's one hundred and twenty-five
          dollars.**

1. How old is the clock?
2. How much is it?
3. How old is the chair?
4. How much is it?
5. How old are the guns?
6. How much are they?
7. How old is the table?
8. How much is it?
9. How old is the phonograph?
10. How much is it?
11. How old are the cups?
12. How much are they?

What time is it?

It's six o'clock.

It's fifteen minutes past eight.
It's (a) quarter past eight.

It's seven o'clock.

It's thirty minutes past eight.
It's half past eight.

It's ten minutes past seven.
It's seven ten.

It's fifteen minutes to ten.
It's (a) quarter to ten.

It's twenty minutes past seven.
It's seven twenty.

It's five minutes to ten.

What time is it?

It's noon.   It's midnight.

Morning is from   Afternoon is   Evening is from
midnight to noon.   from noon to six.   six to midnight.

a   *Answer the following questions about the dialogue.*

1. Why is Mrs. Golo worried?
2. What's her address?
3. Is her house far from the post office?
4. Is the post office on Lime Street?

5. Is it a big fire or a little one?
6. Is Mrs. Golo in the house now?
7. Is it dangerous?

b   *Make commands, using a suitable verb with each of the following words.*

Examples: exercise
     Read/write/repeat the exercise

     Mrs. Golo
     Ask/answer/listen to Mrs. Golo.

1. lesson
2. book
3. door

4. Maria
5. magazine
6. window

7. question
8. Mr. Smith
9. letter

c   *Make commands as indicated.*

Examples: These glasses are dirty. (wash)
     Wash them.

Maria isn't ready. (wait for)
     Wait for her.

1. The door is open. (close)
2. There's Linda. (talk to)
3. Mr. and Mrs. Bascomb are in France. (write to)
4. Albert is at home. (call)

5. I'm your friend. (listen to)
6. Here's Mrs. Golo. (ask)
7. Those cats are hungry. (look at)
8. This orange is good. (eat)
9. Peter is a very good dancer. (dance with)

d   *Change the following sentences as indicated.*

Example: Give Mr. Smith the lamp.
     Please give him the lamp.

1. Take Mrs. Brown these flowers.
2. Write your friends a letter.
3. Bring Tino and me those cards.
4. Give Mrs. Golo a cup of coffee.
5. Bring Mr. Bascomb the newspaper.

6. Take the women those magazines.
7. Give the dog a ball.
8. Write Sam a message.
9. Bring Linda and me a dictionary.

VOCABULARY

across
address (n.)
afternoon
ah
all
answer
ask
away

blackboard
bring

call
candle
class
close (v.)
Coca-Cola
coffee
come
cup

dance (v.)
dangerous

day
department
dictionary
dinner
dish
do
dollar
door
down

each
eat
eighty
emergency
evening

father
fifty
fire
forty

give

go
gun

here
him
house
housewife

immediately

kitchen

lamp
large
laugh
leave
lesson
let
letter
light
listen
little

look (v.)

ma'am
match (n.)
message
midnight
minute
morning
much

near
ninety
noon
now
number
nurse

of
oh
one hundred
open
outside

past
phonograph
please
postcard
price
put

quarter
question

read
ready
repeat
right
room

sandwich
seventy
shelf
sir
sit
sixty

stand
street

take
talk
telephone
them
there
thirty
tonight

up
us

wait (v)
wall
wash
with
worry
write

year

EXPRESSIONS

all right

Have a nice day.

Here you are.

How much is it?

Let's talk.

right away

Don't worry.

Dinner's ready.

My house is on fire.

It's hot in here.

PRONOUNCE THESE WORDS CLEARLY			
e			**iy**
m<u>e</u>n	y<u>e</u>s	h<u>e</u>	m<u>ee</u>t
d<u>e</u>sk	s<u>e</u>ven	sh<u>e</u>	tr<u>ee</u>
th<u>e</u>m	l<u>e</u>tter	w<u>e</u>	str<u>ee</u>t
n<u>e</u>xt	<u>e</u>nvelope	m<u>e</u>	th<u>e</u>se

PRONUNCIATION

s

hat<u>s</u>	pilot<u>s</u>	cup<u>s</u>
coat<u>s</u>	student<u>s</u>	pot<u>s</u>
book<u>s</u>	truck<u>s</u>	clock<u>s</u>
lamp<u>s</u>	street<u>s</u>	desk<u>s</u>

The books and lamps are on the desk.
Give Otis the rabbits and cats.

z

apple<u>s</u>	boy<u>s</u>	pen<u>s</u>
pear<u>s</u>	girl<u>s</u>	letter<u>s</u>
flower<u>s</u>	table<u>s</u>	card<u>s</u>
candle<u>s</u>	chair<u>s</u>	bottle<u>s</u>

Talk to those boys and girls.
Read those letters and magazines.

iz

vas<u>es</u>	bus<u>es</u>	watch<u>es</u>
glass<u>es</u>	nurs<u>es</u>	messag<u>es</u>
dish<u>es</u>	match<u>es</u>	hous<u>es</u>
orang<u>es</u>	dress<u>es</u>	address<u>es</u>

The sandwiches and oranges are for the nurses.
Give them the glasses and dishes, too.

nurses

Those cars, buses, and trucks are new.
Please wash these cups, bottles, and dishes.
The pilots are with the doctors and nurses.

IMPERATIVE

Close the door!
Open the window!

Negative Imperative

Don't	close the door!
	open the window!

With Noun Objects

Look at	Peter. Maria. Barbara and Tino. Johnnie and me. the clock.

With Object Pronouns

Look at	him. her. them. us. it.

With Two Objects

Give	Jimmy Linda the children Albert and me the dog	an apple.

With Object Pronouns

Give	him her them us it	an apple.

Question with HOW MUCH

How much	is the watch?
	are the books?

It's twenty-five dollars.
They're ten dollars.

Question with HOW OLD

How old	is Barbara?
	are the chairs?

She's twenty-four years old.
They're fifteen years old.

TIME

What time is it?

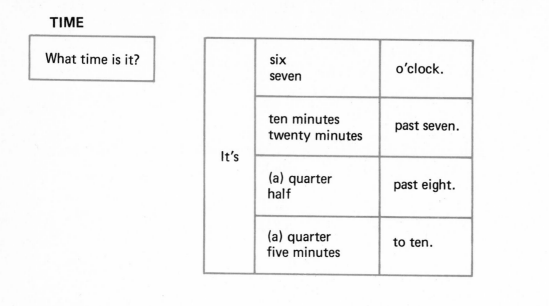

It's	six seven	o'clock.
	ten minutes twenty minutes	past seven.
	(a) quarter half	past eight.
	(a) quarter five minutes	to ten.

NUMBERS 21–100

21	twenty-one	26	twenty-six	31	thirty-one	60	sixty
22	twenty-two	27	twenty-seven	32	thirty-two	70	seventy
23	twenty-three	28	twenty-eight	40	forty	80	eighty
24	twenty-four	29	twenty-nine	41	forty-one	90	ninety
25	twenty-five	30	thirty	50	fifty	100	one hundred

CHAPTER FOUR

Present continuous   **Wh– questions**

a *It's Monday morning. Mr. and Mrs. Bascomb are getting up.*

He's wearing pajamas.

She's wearing a nightgown.

He's brushing his teeth.

_____ her hair.

He's taking a shower.

_____ a bath.

He's making coffee.

_____ tea.

He's putting milk in his coffee.   _____ her tea.

He's reading a magazine.   _____ the newspaper.

He's eating an egg.   _____ an orange.

He's kissing his wife.   _____ her husband.

b

Peter and Maria are sitting
in a snack bar.

Barbara and Tino are sitting
in a coffee shop.

They're watching a football game.

_____

They're drinking Coke.

_____

They're talking to Otis.

_____

They're playing darts.

They're looking at the clock.

They're paying the cashier.

They're saying "goodbye" to Otis.

AFFIRMATIVE

I'm

He's
She's
It's ⎫ eating.

We're
You're
They're

c *Complete the following sentences.*

Example: Albert __'s__ going to the movies.

1. He _____ going with Linda.

2. They _____ leaving now.

3. They _____ saying "goodbye" to Mrs. Brown.

4. She _____ standing in front of the house.

5. Mr. Brown _____ brushing the dog.

6. It _____ sitting on the chair.

7. We _____ waiting for Albert and Linda.

8. I _____ looking at the clock.

NEGATIVE

I'm not

He isn't
She isn't
It isn't ⎫ drinking.

We aren't
You aren't
They aren't

d *Make negative sentences as indicated.*

Example: My friends __aren't__ waiting for the bus.

1. They _____ going to the movies.

2. Johnnie _____ taking a shower.

3. We _____ talking about football.

4. They _____ watching television.

5. I _____ writing a letter.

6. Maria _____ kissing Peter.

7. She _____ looking at him.

8. They _____ talking to the waiter.

9. You _____ eating your dinner.

a

b

a It's Saturday night at the Student Club. Jimmy and Linda are dancing and Tony's watching them. Albert's standing by the table. He's eating a sandwich. Bill and Jane are talking to each other and Karen's walking to the door. It's eleven o'clock and she's going home.

1. What night is it?
2. What are Jimmy and Linda doing? (b)
3. What's Tony doing? (a)
4. Where's Albert standing? (c)
5. What's he eating?
6. What are Bill and Jane doing? (d)
7. What's Karen doing? (e)
8. Where's she going?

b Sam and Mabel Brown are in a small restaurant. They're sitting at a table in the corner. Sam's calling the waiter and Mabel's looking at the menu. The waiter's standing at the counter. He's reading a newspaper.

1. Where are Sam and Mabel?
2. Are they standing or sitting?
3. Who's Sam calling?
4. What's Mabel looking at?
5. Where's the waiter?
6. What's he doing?

AFFIRMATIVE

Karen's walking to the door.
She's _____ .
John's_____ .
He's _____ .

We're reading the newspaper.
They're_____ .
You're _____ .
I'm _____ .

c *Answer the following questions as indicated.*

Example: Is Albert eating an apple? (a sandwich)
     No, he's eating a sandwich.

1. Is Linda dancing with Albert? (with Jimmy)
2. Is Tony watching Karen? (Jimmy and Linda)
3. Is Karen walking to the table? (to the door)
4. Is she going to a movie? (home)
5. Is she wearing a long dress? (a short dress)

1. Are Sam and Mabel sitting in a coffee shop? (in a restaurant)
2. Is Mabel looking at Sam? (at the menu)
3. Is Sam calling the cashier? (the waiter)
4. Is the waiter standing by the table? (by the counter)
5. Is he reading a magazine? (a newspaper)

ALBERT: Hi, Jimmy. Where's your sister?

JIMMY: At home. She's helping my mother.

ALBERT: Is she washing the dishes?

JIMMY: No, she isn't.

ALBERT: What's she doing?

JIMMY: She's cleaning the windows.

ALBERT: Is your father home?

JIMMY: Yes. He's cutting the grass.

ALBERT: Why aren't you working, too?

JIMMY: It's Sunday. I'm resting today.

INTERROGATIVE

Is Linda washing the dishes ?	Are Albert and Jimmy working now ?
— she _____ ?	— your friends _____ ?
— Mr. Brown _____ ?	— they _____ ?
— he _____ ?	— you _____ ?

d   *Make questions as indicated.*

Examples: Linda is helping her mother.   (cleaning the windows)
           Is she cleaning the windows?

           Mr. and Mrs. Brown are at home.   (watching television)
           Are they watching television?

1. Mr. and Mrs. Bascomb are in the kitchen.   (washing the dishes)
2. Mrs. Bascomb is sitting down.   (reading a book)
3. She's having breakfast.   (eating an egg)
4. Mr. Bascomb is standing up.   (looking at his watch)
5. He's leaving the room.   (saying "goodbye")

1. Barbara and Tino are in a coffee shop.   (calling the waiter)
2. The waiter is coming.   (bringing the menu)
3. They're ordering breakfast.   (asking for coffee and eggs)
4. Barbara is very pretty today.   (wearing a new dress)
5. She's brushing her hair.   (looking in the mirror)

NEGATIVE

Linda isn't washing the dishes.	Albert and Jimmy aren't working now.
She _____.	Your friends _____.
Mr. Brown _____.	They _____.
He _____.	You _____.

e   *Make negative sentences as indicated.*

Examples: Albert and Jimmy are talking about Linda.   (Karen)
           They aren't talking about Karen.

           Mr. Brown is listening to the radio.   (his wife)
           He isn't listening to his wife.

1. Mr. and Mrs. Bascomb are having breakfast.   (dinner)
2. Mrs. Bascomb is reading a newspaper.   (a book)
3. She's eating an orange.   (an egg)
4. Mr. Bascomb is looking at his watch.   (his wife)
5. He's saying "goodbye."   ("hello")

1. Barbara and Tino are calling the waiter.   (the cashier)
2. The waiter is bringing the menu.   (the bill)
3. They're asking for coffee and eggs.   (tea and sandwiches)
4. Barbara is wearing a new dress.   (an old dress)
5. She's brushing her hair.   (her teeth)

The Brown family is in the park. It's a beautiful Sunday and the sun is shining. Mr. Brown is smoking a pipe and reading a book. Mrs. Brown is preparing lunch. She's making sandwiches and lemonade. Linda is sitting by a tree drawing pictures. Jimmy is playing football. An old man is sitting on the hill watching the game. He's smiling and thinking about the past.

a   *Answer the following questions about the story.*

1. Where is the Brown family?
2. What day of the week is it?
3. Is Mr. Brown reading a magazine?
4. Is he smoking a pipe or a cigar?
5. Is Mrs. Brown preparing breakfast?
6. What's she making?
7. Where's Linda sitting?
8. What's she doing?
9. Is Jimmy playing basketball?
10. What is the old man doing?

b   *Make original sentences with these words.*

Examples: We/clean/kitchen
   We're cleaning the kitchen.

Anne/help/us
Anne's helping us.

1. Mrs. Golo/eat/apple
2. Mr. Golo/make/sandwich
3. They/drink/coffee
4. They/wash/dishes
5. Tino/write/letter
6. He/listen/radio
7. Barbara/brush/teeth
8. She/wear/pajamas
9. I/read/magazine
10. You/play/guitar

c   *Change the following sentences to the negative.*

Examples: She's calling the hospital.
   She isn't calling the hospital.

We're going to the park.
We aren't going to the park.

1. He's buying a house.
2. She's working at the library.
3. They're going to a party.
4. They're waiting for Nancy.
5. She's writing a letter.
6. He's listening to the radio.
7. They're watching television.
8. She's preparing dinner.
9. He's reading a book.

d   *Make questions as indicated.*

Examples: Mr. Brown is at home. (watch/television)
   Is he watching television?

Jimmy is in the bathroom. (take/shower)
Is he taking a shower?

1. Mrs. Brown is in the kitchen. (make/tea)
2. Linda is in her room. (read/book)
3. Albert is in the park. (play/football)
4. Barney is in a restaurant. (eat/dinner)
5. Nancy is at home. (write/letter)
6. Mr. Bascomb is in his office. (smoke/cigar)
7. Barbara is at a party. (wear/red dress)
8. Fred is at the snack bar. (drink/coffee)
9. Maria is at the antique shop. (buy/vase)

e *Make questions with* **who**, **what**, *or* **where**, *as indicated.*

Examples: Albert's going <u>to the movies</u>.
Where's he going?

He's talking to <u>Linda</u>.
Who's he talking to?

The children are playing <u>in the park</u>.
Where are they playing?

They're looking at <u>the birds</u>.
What are they looking at?

1. Barney's reading <u>a magazine</u>.
2. He's waiting for <u>Nancy</u>.
3. He's sitting in <u>a coffee shop</u>.
4. Maria's talking to <u>Peter</u>.
5. They're standing <u>at the bus stop</u>.

6. They're eating <u>sandwiches</u>.
7. Mrs. Brown's watching <u>television</u>.
8. She's sitting <u>in the living room</u>.
9. She's calling <u>Mr. Brown</u>.

f *Answer the following questions using object pronouns.*

Example: Is Peter asking <u>the waiter</u> for a glass of water? (a menu)
No, he's asking <u>him</u> for a menu.

a telegram

1. Is Tino taking <u>Barbara</u> a magazine? (a book)
2. Is Mrs. Brown giving <u>the children</u> a cat? (a dog)
3. Is Linda asking <u>her father</u> for a clock? (a watch)
4. Is Albert writing <u>Linda</u> a letter? (a postcard)
5. Is Otis bringing <u>the boys</u> a football? (a basketball)
6. Is Maria giving <u>Peter</u> an apple? (a pear)
7. Is Jimmy bringing <u>his mother</u> a chair? (a table)
8. Is Anne taking <u>Mr. Bascomb</u> a letter? (a telegram)
9. Is Mrs. Golo giving <u>the students</u> a dictionary? (an encyclopedia)

an encyclopedia

g *Complete the following sentences with suitable prepositions.*

Example: Mr. Brown is sitting ___*in*___ the living room.

1. He's writing a letter _____ his brother _____ New York.

2. Barbara's going _____ the movies _____ Tino.

3. Albert's standing _____ the bus stop.

4. He's thinking _____ Linda.

5. She's walking _____ the library _____ Jimmy.

6. Barney's having lunch _____ Nancy _____ a Mexican restaurant.

7. They're sitting _____ a table _____ the corner.

8. Barney's talking _____ the waiter _____ football.

9. Nancy's drinking a cup _____ coffee and smiling _____ Barney.

VOCABULARY

about	Coke	goodbye	milk	prepare	tea
antique shop	counter	grass	mirror		teeth
	cut (v.)	green	Monday	radio	telegram
basketball			mother	rest (v.)	television
bath	darts	hair		restaurant	think
bathroom	draw	help	night		today
beach	drink (v.)	husband	nightgown	say	
bill				shine	walk (v.)
breakfast	encyclopedia	kiss	pajamas	shower	water
brother			park	sing	wear
brush (v.)	family	lemonade	party	sister	week
buy	football	long	pay	smile (v.)	wife
	for	lunch	picture	smoke (v.)	
cashier			pipe	snack bar	
cigar	game	make	play (v.)	sun	
coffee shop	get	menu	policeman	Sunday	

PRONUNCIATION

i		
give	dish	big
him	with	kiss
this	it	sit
little	rich	kitchen

iy		
we	beach	meet
tea	cheap	please
street	eat	read
clean	leave	green

Give Nick this picture.
His little sister is in the kitchen.

Please meet the teacher at the museum.
The streets are clean and the tea is green.

Jimmy is cleaning the windows.
He isn't reading his magazine.

PRESENT CONTINUOUS   Affirmative

He She It	's (is)	
I	'm (am)	watching television.
You We They	're (are)	

Negative

He She It	isn't (is not) 's not	
I	'm not (am not)	watching television.
You We They	aren't (are not) 're not	

Interrogative

Is	he she it	
Am	I	watching television?
Are	you we they	

Short Answers

Yes,	he she it	is.
	I	am.
	you we they	are.

No,	he she it	isn't.
	I	'm not.
	you we they	aren't.

Question with
WHAT, WHO, WHERE

Albert is eating <u>a sandwich</u>.	What 's (is) he eating?	A sandwich.
Linda is dancing with <u>Jimmy</u>.	Who 's (is) she dancing with?	Jimmy.
Sam is going <u>to the garage</u>.	Where 's (is) he going?	To the garage.

CHAPTER FIVE

"To have"
Possessive
adjectives

Possessive of
nouns
"Whose . . .?"

MRS. GOLO: You have a nice husband, Mabel.

MRS. BROWN: Yes, and he has a good wife.

MRS. GOLO: You have beautiful children.

MRS. BROWN: Yes, and they have a good mother.

MRS. GOLO: You have a wonderful family.

MRS. BROWN: That's right. We have everything.

MRS. GOLO: No, Mabel. There's one thing
                you don't have.

MRS. BROWN: What's that?

MRS. GOLO: Humility!

AFFIRMATIVE

You have a nice family.   Peter has a good job.
They_____.   He _____.
We _____.   Maria_____.
I _____.   She_____.

a *Complete the following sentences with **have** or **has**.*

Examples: Barney ___*has*___ a red taxi.

Mr. and Mrs. Brown ___*have*___ a large refrigerator.

1. They _____ a friend named Jack.

2. He _____ two brothers.

3. You _____ a nice family.

4. Tino _____ a girlfriend named Barbara.

5. She _____ a job at the bank.

6. We _____ a good library.

7. I _____ a new radio.

8. Mrs. Bascomb _____ an intelligent husband.

9. He _____ an important job.

10. They _____ an expensive car.

a refrigerator

a radio

b *Ask and answer questions as indicated.*

Example: a brother
        Student A: Do you have a brother?
        Student B: Yes, I do. OR No, I don't.

1. a sister   6. a guitar
2. a clock   7. a record player
3. a watch   8. a camera
4. a cat   9. a football
5. a dog   10. a bicycle

a record player   a camera

ANNE: Barbara, give me your pen, please.

BARBARA: I don't have a pen. Here's a pencil.

ANNE: Thank you. Do you have a piece of paper?

BARBARA: Here you are. Is it for a letter?

ANNE: That's right. Do you have an envelope?

BARBARA: Yes. But I don't have stamps.

ANNE: That's O.K. I have stamps.

BARBARA: Oh, really? That's good.

INTERROGATIVE

Do you have an envelope ?   Does Anne have a pen ?
___ they_____ ?   _____ she_____ ?
___ we _____ ?   _____ John_____ ?
___ the girls _____ ?   _____ he _____ ?

c   *Complete these questions.*

Examples: ___*Do*_____ they have a typewriter?

___*Does*_____ Albert have a telephone?

a typewriter   a telephone

1. _____ we have a dictionary?   6. _____ you have a guitar?

2. _____ she have a bicycle?   7. _____ Maria have a brown hat?

3. _____ you have a sister?   8. _____ they have an apartment?

4. _____ I have your address?   9. _____ he have a lamp?

5. _____ Nick have a garage?

NEGATIVE

We don't have a clock.   Linda doesn't have a car.
They_____ .   Jimmy _____ .
You _____ .   He _____ .
I _____ .   Mrs. Golo _____ .

d   *Make negative sentences as indicated.*

Examples: They have a guitar. (a piano)
But they don't have a piano.

Mrs. Golo has a radio. (a television)
But she doesn't have a television.

a piano

1. We have a library. (a museum)
2. Barbara has a pencil. (a pen)
3. I have a sister. (a brother)
4. She has a hat. (an umbrella)
5. Jimmy has a football. (a basketball)
6. We have a table. (a desk)
7. She has a dog. (a cat)
8. They have an office. (a telephone)
9. He has a job. (a car)

a television (TV)

e *Look at the pictures and answer the following questions.*

Does Tino have
a wallet?

Yes, he does.

Does Mrs. Bascomb
have a wallet?

No, she doesn't.
She has a handbag.

Does Maria have
a bottle?

Does Barbara have
a typewriter?

Does Albert have
an apple?

Does Simon have
a rabbit?

Does Mrs. Golo
have an umbrella?

Does Barney have
a truck?

Does Anne have
a guitar?

f *Look at the picture and answer the following questions.*

Examples: Do Mr. and Mrs. Wankie have a house?
No, they don't. (They have an apartment.)

Do they have a telephone?
Yes, they do.

1. Do they have a record player?
2. Do they have a piano?
3. Do they have a clock?
4. Do they have a bookcase?
5. Do they have a typewriter?
6. Do they have a camera?
7. Do they have a television?
8. Do they have a dog?
9. Do they have a cat?

POSSESSIVE
ADJECTIVES

I have a book.	It's my book.
You have a book.	It's your book.
He has a book.	It's his book.
She has a book.	It's her book.
We have a book.	It's our book.
They have a book.	It's their book.

a *Complete the following sentences with* **my, your, his, her, our, or their.**

Example: Peter has a clock in ____*his*____ apartment.

1. Maria has a piano in _____ apartment.

2. Mr. and Mrs. Brown have a television in _____ living room.

3. I have an umbrella in _____ car.

4. We have a good library in _____ city.

5. She has a radio in _____ room.

6. You have a beautiful vase in _____ kitchen.

7. I have a pen in _____ pocket.

8. He has a newspaper in _____ desk.

b *Complete the following sentences.*

Example: They're painting ____*their*____ house.

1. I'm waiting for _____ sister.

2. She's talking with _____ friends.

3. They're doing _____ homework.

4. Is Jimmy helping _____ mother?

5. Linda is talking with _____ father.

6. He's cleaning _____ shoes.

7. Are you thinking about _____ family?

8. We're thinking about _____ friends.

JIMMY:	Whose car is that?
ALBERT:	It's Mr. Smith's car.
JIMMY:	It's beautiful, isn't it?
ALBERT:	It sure is.

c *Answer the following questions as indicated.*

Examples: Whose car is that? (Mr. Smith)   Whose pens are these? (Nancy)
     It's Mr. Smith's car.   **They're Nancy's pens.**

1. Whose watch is this? (Linda)
2. Whose lamp is that? (Mr. Bascomb)
3. Whose envelopes are those? (Barbara)
4. Whose magazines are these? (Tino)
5. Whose ball is this? (the dog)
6. Whose glasses are these? (Mrs. Golo)

d *Answer the following questions as indicated.*

Examples: Whose bicycles are those? (the girls)   Whose house is that? (the Browns)
     They're the girls' bicycles.   **It's the Browns' house.**

1. Whose football is this? (the boys)
2. Whose books are these? (the students)
3. Whose car is that? (the Golos)
4. Whose offices are those? (the doctors)
5. Whose letters are these? (the girls)
6. Whose apartment is that? (the Wilsons)

e   *Look at the pictures and complete the following sentences as indicated.*

Mr. Brown is a family man. He has a wife, Mabel, and two children. Their names are Jimmy and Linda. The Browns have a small house with a red roof. Their house is near the library. Mr. Brown has a Volkswagen and his wife also has a Volkswagen. His car is red and her car is blue. Right now, Mr. Brown is washing his car. Mrs. Brown is working in the garden. She's planting vegetables. Linda is helping her mother in the garden. Jimmy isn't home. He's playing football with his friends.

a   *Answer the following questions about the story.*

1. Does Mr. Brown have children?
2. What are their names?
3. Do the Browns have a large house with a white roof?
4. Where is their house?
5. What kind of car does Mr. Brown have?
6. What color is his car?
7. What color is Mrs. Brown's car?
8. Do the Browns have a garden?
9. What's Mr. Brown doing now?
10. What's Mrs. Brown doing?
11. What's Linda doing?
12. Is Jimmy helping, too?

b   *Answer the following questions using short answers.*

Examples: Does Tino have a girlfriend named Maria?
No, he doesn't.

Does he have a girlfriend named Barbara?
Yes, he does.

1. Does Sam Brown have a white hat?
2. Does he have a big car?
3. Does Jimmy have a sister named Linda?
4. Does she have blond hair?
5. Does Barbara have blond hair?
6. Does Nick have a restaurant?
7. Does he have a garage?
8. Does Barney have a taxi?
9. Does Maria have a taxi?

c   *Make questions as indicated.*

Examples: Mr. and Mrs. Golo don't have a daughter.   (a son)
Do they have a son?

Otis doesn't have a radio.   (a television)
Does he have a television?

1. They don't have a desk.   (a table)
2. Barbara doesn't have a pen.   (a pencil)
3. We don't have a French dictionary.   (a Spanish dictionary)
4. He doesn't have a hat.   (a coat)
5. They don't have a cat.   (a dog)
6. Barney doesn't have a clock.   (a watch)
7. He doesn't have a wife.   (a girlfriend)
8. They don't have a house.   (an apartment)
9. She doesn't have a piano.   (a guitar)

d *Complete the following sentences.*

Example: What do you have in _*your*_ car?

1. What does she have in _____ handbag?

2. What do they have in _____ kitchen?

3. What does he have in _____ pocket?

4. What do we have in _____ garden?

5. What does Maria have in _____ room?

6. What do you have in _____ apartment?

7. What do the Browns have in _____ garage?

8. What does Peter have in _____ office?

9. What do you have in _____ wallet?

e *Change the following sentences using the possessive adjective.*

Example: You have an interesting job. _*Your job is interesting.*_

1. We have a wonderful library. _____

2. I have a new camera. _____

3. She has an Italian boyfriend. _____

4. They have expensive dictionaries. _____

5. You have an intelligent sister. _____

6. Mrs. Brown has a wonderful family. _____

7. Albert has a black umbrella. _____

8. We have a small apartment. _____

9. You have a beautiful garden. _____

f *Make questions as indicated.*

Examples: Look at that car.
      Whose car is it?

Look at those bicycles.
      Whose bicycles are they?

1. Look at that gun.
2. Look at this hat.
3. Look at these stamps.

4. Look at those flowers.
5. Look at that dog.
6. Look at these books.

7. Look at this dress.
8. Look at that camera.
9. Look at those pictures.

g *Write a short composition describing your family.*

VOCABULARY

also	garden	kind	piece	their
apartment	girlfriend		pocket	thing
		name (v.)		TV
boyfriend	handbag		really	typewriter
brown	have	O.K.	record player	
but	homework	our	refrigerator	uncle
	humility		roof	
camera		paint (v.)		vegetable
	important	paper	son	
daughter	interesting	pen	stamp (n.)	wallet
		pencil		white
everything	job	piano	taxi	whose
				wonderful

EXPRESSIONS

What kind is it?   Oh, really?   That's good.   of course   right now

PRONUNCIATION

æ				e		
happy	class	ask		red	telephone	ready
sad	handbag	man		desk	expensive	envelope
glad	stand	candle		bed	dress	television
bad	lamp	camera		pen	letter	message

Nancy has a black hat.
The happy dancer is laughing at the fat cat.

The red dress is very expensive.
Fred's letter is in the envelope.

Ellen has a telegram in her handbag.
The black hat is next to the red lamp.

TO HAVE　Affirmative

He She	has	a car.
I You We They	have	

Negative

He She	doesn't (does not)	have a car.
I You We They	don't (do not)	

Interrogative

Does	he she	have a car?
Do	I you we they	

Short Answers

Yes,	he she	does.
	I you we they	do.

No,	he she	doesn't.
	I you we they	don't.

POSSESSIVE ADJECTIVES

It's	my your our their his her	house.

Questions with WHOSE

Whose	radio is this?
	pens are these?

Whose	house is that?
	bicycles are those?

POSSESSIVE OF NOUNS

It's Mrs. Golo's radio.

They're Linda's pens.

It's the Browns' house.

They're the girls' bicycles.

CHAPTER SIX

"There is"/ "there are"
Uncountables

"To want" and "to like"
Possessive pronouns

a   There's a dog under the table.
_____ chair by the table.
_____ typewriter on the table.
_____ lamp behind the typewriter.
_____ vase next to the typewriter.
_____ rose in the vase.
_____ cup in front of the vase.

b   There are some cars in the street.
_____ people at the bus stop.
_____ birds on the sidewalk.
_____ bicycles under the tree.
_____ children in front of the theater.
_____ tables and chairs on the sidewalk.

c   *Answer the following questions, using short answers.*

Examples: Is there a typewriter on the table?   Is there a book on the table?
          Yes, there is.   **No, there isn't.**

1. Is there a cup on the table?
2. Is there a glass on the table?
3. Is there a bottle on the table?
4. Is there a vase on the table?
5. Is there a rose in the vase?
6. Is there a chair by the table?
7. Is there a magazine on the chair?
8. Is there a dog under the table?
9. Is there a cat under the table?

d   *Answer the following questions as indicated.*

Examples: Are there any cars in the street?   Are there any buses in the street?
          Yes, there are.   **No, there aren't.**

1. Are there any trucks in the street?
2. Are there any people at the bus stop?
3. Are there any people at Joe's Cafe?
4. Are there any birds on the sidewalk?
5. Are there any birds in the tree?
6. Are there any bicycles under the tree?
7. Are there any tables and chairs on the sidewalk?
8. Are there any glasses on the tables?
9. Are there any children in front of the theater?

e   *Answer the following questions.*

Example: How many cars are there in the street?
         There are three cars in the street.

1. How many people are there at the bus stop?
2. How many birds are there on the sidewalk?
3. How many bicycles are there under the tree?
4. How many chairs are there on the sidewalk?
5. How many tables are there on the sidewalk?
6. How many children are there in front of the theater?

1. How many days are there in a week?
2. How many months are there in a year?
3. How many hours are there in a day?
4. How many minutes are there in an hour?
5. How many people are there in your family?
6. How many pages are there in this book?

f *Complete the following sentences about the picture.*

1. There's a bus in the street. It's a school bus.
2. _____ garden in the front yard. _____ vegetable garden.
3. _____ fence around the garden. _____ wire fence.
4. _____ table near the garden. _____ picnic table.

1. There are some cans on the sidewalk. They're trash cans.
2. _____ trees next to the house. _____ peach trees.
3. _____ bottles on the table. _____ milk bottles.
4. _____ boots on the steps. _____ cowboy boots.

g *Answer the following questions about the picture.*

Examples: What is there in the street?
There's a bus in the street.

What kind of bus is it?
It's a school bus.

What is there on the sidewalk?
There are some cans on the sidewalk.

What kind of cans are they?
They're trash cans.

1. What is there next to the house?
   What kind of trees are they?
2. What is there in the front yard?
   What kind of garden is it?
3. What is there around the garden?
   What kind of fence is it?

4. What is there near the garden?
   What kind of table is it?
5. What is there on the table?
   What kind of bottles are they?
6. What is there on the steps?
   What kind of boots are they?

UNCOUNTABLES

There's some bread on the table.
_____ cheese _____ .
_____ butter _____ .
_____ milk _____ .

h   *Ask and answer questions about the pictures, as in the example.*

STUDENT A:

What's in the bottle?

STUDENT B:

There's some milk in the bottle.

a bottle of milk

a pitcher of lemonade

a bowl of soup

a box of cereal

a jar of mustard

a cup of coffee

a dish of ice cream

a can of tomato juice

i *Complete the following sentences with* **there's a**, **there's some**, *or* **there are some**.

Examples: ___*There's a*___ plate on the table.

___*There are some*___ cookies on the plate.

1. _____ coffeepot on the table.

_____ coffee in the coffeepot.

2. _____ bread on the table.

_____ knives next to the bread.

3. _____ bottle on the table.

_____ milk in the bottle.

4. _____ sandwiches on the table.

_____ cheese next to the sandwiches.

5. _____ dish on the table.

_____ cherries in the dish.

Note: knife → knives   wife → wives   life → lives

WAITRESS: What do you want for lunch, sir?

PETER SMITH: I want some coffee and a ham
                 sandwich.

WAITRESS: Do you want mayonnaise on your
                 sandwich?

PETER SMITH: No, thank you. I don't like
                 mayonnaise.

WAITRESS: Do you like mustard?

PETER SMITH: Yes, I do. And give me some
                 ketchup, please.

WAITRESS: Yes, sir. Here's a bottle of
                 ketchup.

PETER SMITH: Thank you very much.

AFFIRMATIVE

Peter likes ketchup.	They like lemonade.
He _____ .	We _____ .
Maria _____ .	You _____ .
She _____ .	I _____ .

a *Make sentences as indicated.*

Example: Peter likes ketchup. (a bottle of ketchup)
  He wants a bottle of ketchup.

1. He likes coffee. (a cup of coffee)
2. Linda likes milk. (a glass of milk)
3. She likes ice cream. (a dish of ice cream)
4. Tino likes tomato juice. (a can of tomato juice)

Example: I like cake. (a piece of cake)
  I want a piece of cake.

1. They like wine. (a bottle of wine)
2. I like bread. (a slice of bread)
3. We like soup. (a bowl of soup)
4. They like French fries. (a plate of French fries)

a piece of cake

a slice of bread

a plate of
French fries
(fried potatoes)

NEGATIVE

Peter doesn't like mayonnaise.	They don't like Coke.
He _____ .	We _____ .
Maria _____ .	You _____ .
She _____ .	I _____ .

b *Make the following sentences negative.*

Examples: Peter likes mustard. (mayonnaise)
  But he doesn't like mayonnaise.

  Mr. and Mrs. Bascomb like French food. (English food)
  But they don't like English food.

1. They like New York. (Chicago)
2. He likes opera. (ballet)
3. She likes Mr. Poole. (his wife)
4. Barbara and Tino like tomato juice. (tomato soup)
5. He likes coffee. (tea)
6. She likes spaghetti. (pizza)
7. We like oranges. (pears)
8. Albert likes chocolate ice cream. (chocolate cake)
9. I like tomatoes. (potatoes)

POSSESSIVE ADJECTIVES	POSSESSIVE PRONOUNS
my	mine
your	yours
his	his
her	hers
our	ours
their	theirs

c   *Make sentences with **mine, yours, his, hers, ours,** or **theirs,** as indicated.*

Examples: This is your book. _This book is yours._

These are their typewriters. _These typewriters are theirs._

1. This is my hat. _____

2. That's his radio. _____

3. These are our magazines. _____

4. This is her handbag. _____

5. That's their camera. _____

6. This is my dog and that's her dog. _____

7. This is our desk. _____

8. Those are your pens. _____

d   *Answer in the negative.*

Examples: Is this your umbrella? _No, it isn't mine._

Are those his pictures? _No, they aren't his._

1. Is this his radio? _____

2. Is that her dictionary? _____

3. Is that your car? _____

4. Are those our coats? _____

5. Are these her pencils? _____

6. Is that his chair? _____

7. Is that their apartment? _____

8. Is this our typewriter? _____

There's an old white house on Bunker Hill. It's a traditional American house.
It has large windows and a wide green door. There's a statue of a woman in
front of the house. And there are red roses in the garden. The trees behind
the house are tall and very beautiful. The house belongs to an old professor.
He's a butterfly expert. His name is Dr. Pasto. The people of Bunker Hill like
him. He's very friendly. He has visitors every day. At the moment, Dr. Pasto
is chasing butterflies. He wants them for his collection.

a   *Answer the following questions.*

1. What's on Bunker Hill?
2. What kind of house is it?
3. What color is the door?
4. Is there a statue of a man in front of the house?
5. What's in the garden?

6. Where are the trees?
7. What are they like?
8. Who does the house belong to?
9. Do the people of Bunker Hill like him?
10. What's Dr. Pasto doing now?
11. Why does he want butterflies?

b   *Look at the picture above and answer the following questions.*

Examples: What's in the bathroom?   (a mirror)
   There's a mirror in the bathroom.

   What's in the bedroom?   (some flowers)
   There are some flowers in the bedroom.

1. What's in the kitchen?   (a stove)
   (some pots)
   (a sink)
2. What's in the living room?   (some chairs)
   (a table)
   (a television)
3. What's in the bathroom?   (a bathtub)
   (a toilet)
   (a wash basin)
4. What's in the bedroom?   (a bed)
   (some flowers)
   (a picture)

c   *Make sentences with **there's a**, **there's some**, or **there are some**.*

Examples: I'm looking for some ketchup.   (on the table)
There's some ketchup on the table.

I'm looking for some magazines.   (in the living room)
There are some magazines in the living room.

1. I'm looking for a dictionary.   (in the library)
2. I'm looking for some milk.   (in the kitchen)
3. I'm looking for some pencils.   (in the desk)
4. I'm looking for an umbrella.   (on the chair)
5. I'm looking for some stamps.   (in the envelope)
6. I'm looking for some paper.   (on the table)
7. I'm looking for a mirror.   (in the bathroom)
8. I'm looking for some matches.   (in the handbag)

d   *Change the following sentences from singular to plural as indicated.*

Example: There's a book on the desk. It's a French book.

There are some books on the desk. They're French books.

1. There's an orange in the bowl. It's a small orange.

   _____

2. There's a flower in the vase. It's a pretty flower.

   _____

3. There's a candle by the window. It's a white candle.

   _____

4. There's a newspaper in the car. It's an old newspaper.

   _____

5. There's a bicycle under the tree. It's a new bicycle.

   _____

6. There's a rose in the garden. It's a yellow rose.

   _____

7. There's a tree behind the house. It's a beautiful tree.

   _____

8. There's an apple on the table. It's a red apple.

   _____

e   *Answer the following questions in the negative.*

Examples: Is Linda drinking coffee?
No. She doesn't like coffee.

Are the Browns planting tomatoes?
No. They don't like tomatoes.

1. Is Albert playing basketball?
2. Are Peter and Maria eating spaghetti?
3. Is Dr. Pasto watching television?
4. Is Mrs. Golo listening to rock music?
5. Are they drinking tea?
6. Is Peter asking for mayonnaise?
7. Are Mr. and Mrs. Bascomb going to the beach?
8. Is Barney drinking milk?
9. Is Nancy eating chocolate cake?

f   *Answer the following questions about yourself.*

1. Are you thirsty?
2. Do you want a glass of water?
3. Are you hungry?
4. Do you want a sandwich?
5. Do you like ice cream?
6. Do you like lemonade?
7. What's your favorite sport?
8. Do you like football?
9. What kind of music do you like?

g   *Make questions as indicated.*

Examples: Nick and Barney don't like basketball. (football)
Do they like football?

Barbara doesn't have a car. (a bicycle)
Does she have a bicycle?

1. Nancy doesn't like apple juice. (orange juice)
2. Jimmy and Linda don't have a cat. (a dog)
3. They don't want a new television. (a new radio)
4. Dr. Pasto doesn't have a stamp collection. (a butterfly collection)
5. Maria doesn't like red roses. (yellow roses)
6. Albert doesn't want cake. (ice cream)
7. Mr. and Mrs. Bascomb don't like rock music. (classical music)
8. Anne doesn't have a job at the library. (a job at the bank)
9. She doesn't want a new hat. (a new dress)

h   *Make sentences with **mine, yours, his, hers, ours,** or **theirs.***

Examples: This is my chair. *This chair is mine.*

Those are her photographs. *Those photographs are hers.*

1. That's our dictionary. _____

2. This is his notebook. _____

3. That's their table. _____

4. Those are your stamps. _____

5. These are my envelopes. _____

6. This is our typewriter. _____

7. That's her handbag. _____

8. Those are my magazines. _____

9. These are his cards. _____

10. This is your umbrella. _____

i   *Complete the following sentences, using suitable prepositions.*

Example: Barbara is sitting *with* Tino *in* his car.

1. They're talking _____ her job _____ the bank.

2. Albert and Linda are sitting _____ a coffee shop.

3. She wants a bowl _____ soup _____ lunch.

4. Jimmy is buying stamps _____ the post office _____ Maple Street.

5. He's writing a letter _____ a friend _____ Florida.

6. That old house belongs _____ Dr. Pasto.

7. He's working _____ his friends _____ the garden.

8. I'm giving this butterfly _____ Dr. Pasto _____ his collection.

j   *Write a short composition describing your house or apartment.*

VOCABULARY

any	chase	ham	notebook	slice (n.)	watch (v.)
around	cheese	hour		some	why
	cherry		opera	soup	wide
bathtub	chocolate	ice cream		spaghetti	wine
bed	classical		page	sport	wire
bedroom	coffeepot	jar	people	statue	
belong	collection	juice	photograph	step (n.)	yard
boot	cookie		picnic	stove	yellow
bowl		ketchup	pitcher		
box	Dr.	knife	pizza	theater	
bread			plant (v.)	toilet	
butter	every	life	plate	tomato	
butterfly	expert	like (v.)	potato	traditional	
by			professor	trash	
	fence	mayonnaise			
cafe	food	mine	rock music	visitor	
cake	French fries	moment	rose		
can (n.)	fried	month		waitress	
cereal	friendly	music	sidewalk	want	
	front	mustard	sink (n.)	wash basin	

EXPRESSIONS

Thank you very much.   What kind of house is it?

PRONUNCIATION

	ay			ey	
time	buy	mine	cake	vase	make
write	pipe	by	paper	bookcase	take
shine	white	slice	airplane	favorite	eight
bicycle	pilot	like	plate	chase	game

Simon's pipe is by the typewriter.   Take the vase and the plates to Miss Paine.
The white bicycle is behind the library.   Mabel is making a cake today.

I'm waiting for an airplane pilot.
Jane likes cake and ice cream.

THERE IS/THERE ARE Affirmative

There's (There is)	a bottle	
There are	some glasses	on the table.
There's (There is)	some cake	

It's	a large bottle.
They're (They are)	small glasses.
It's	chocolate cake.

Interrogative

Is there	a bottle	
Are there	any glasses	on the table?
Is there	any cake	

Short answers

	there is.
Yes,	there are.
	there is.

	there isn't.
No,	there aren't.
	there isn't.

Question with HOW MANY

How many	bottles glasses	are there?

There's There are	one (bottle). five (glasses).

POSSESSIVE ADJECTIVES

It's	my your our their his her	house.

POSSESSIVE PRONOUNS

It's	mine. yours. ours. theirs. his. hers.

NOUNS AS MODIFIERS

It's a	school bus. business letter.
They're	apple trees. office buildings.

WANT Affirmative

He She	wants	a glass of water.
I You We They	want	

Negative

He She	doesn't (does not)	want a glass of water.
I You We They	don't (do not)	

Interrogative

Does	he she	want a glass of water?
Do	I you we they	

Short answers

Yes,	he she	does.
	I you we they	do.

No,	he she	doesn't.
	I you we they	don't.

CHAPTER SEVEN

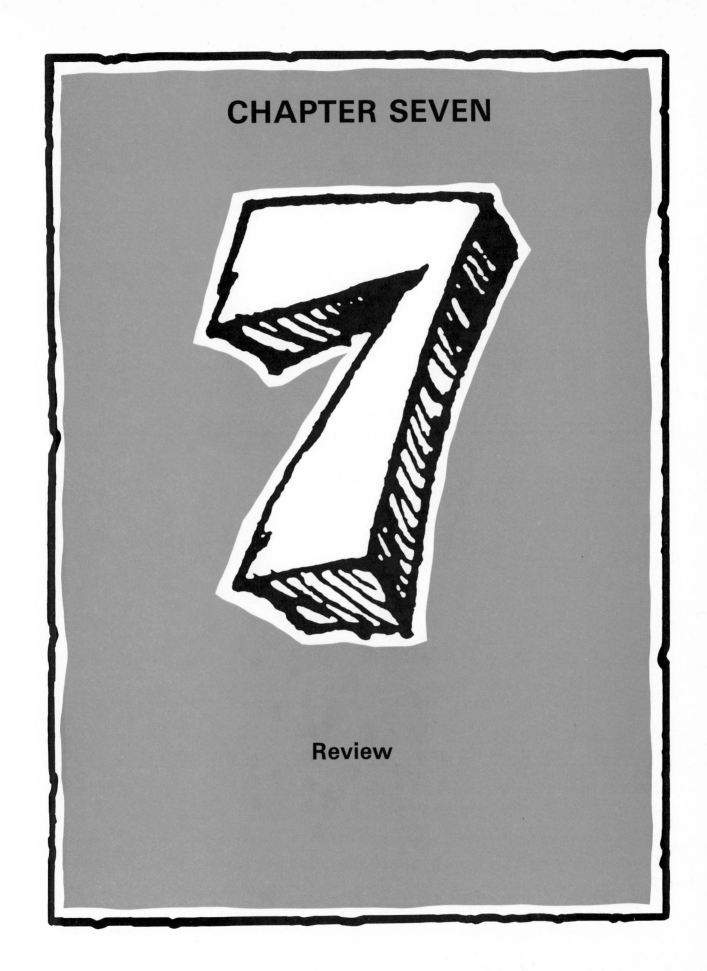

Review

THE ART EXHIBITION

Today there's an art exhibition in City Park. Otis Jackson has some of his new paintings in the exhibition. He's showing them to the public for the first time. Otis is a very good artist. His paintings are an expression of his strong personality. He's a vegetarian; that's why Otis paints fruit and vegetables. He's also a Sagittarian; his birthday is in December. Sagittarians are intelligent people, and they like unusual things. The fruit and vegetables in Otis's paintings are different from ordinary fruit and vegetables. They're very large and have strange shapes and colors.

At the moment Otis is talking to some art lovers, including Dr. Pasto. They're standing around some of his paintings of fruit. Otis is a good talker, and he has some interesting ideas on art.

"Art is life," says Otis. "My paintings are me."

"That's certainly true," says Dr. Pasto. "You and your paintings are very original."

"Thank you, Dr. Pasto."

"This is a fine painting here, Otis. The colors are beautiful."

"You're looking at one of my favorite compositions. It's called 'The Happy Butterfly.' "

"Is it for sale, Otis?"

"Yes, sir."

"How much do you want for it?"

"I'm asking eighty dollars."

"Let's see. I think I have eighty dollars in my wallet. Yes. Here you are, Otis."

"Thank you, Dr. Pasto. You have a good painting there. Enjoy it."

a *Answer the following questions about the story.*

1. Where's the art exhibition?
2. Does Otis have his new paintings in the exhibition?
3. Is he an ordinary artist?
4. Does Otis like meat?
5. Why does he paint fruit and vegetables?
6. Is Otis a Sagittarian?
7. When is his birthday?
8. What are the fruit and vegetables in Otis's paintings like?
9. Who is Otis talking to?
10. What does Otis say about art?
11. What is Dr. Pasto looking at?
12. How much does Otis want for the painting?

b *Change the following sentences from singular to plural.*

Examples: That's an old bicycle.
Those are old bicycles.

This glass is clean.
These glasses are clean.

1. That's a French cigarette.
2. This is a cheap dress.
3. This butterfly is beautiful.
4. That painting is expensive.
5. That's a new radio.

6. This is a good camera.
7. This window is dirty.
8. That boy is intelligent.
9. That's an unusual woman.

c *Answer the following questions using opposites.*

Examples: Is Mr. Bascomb poor?
No, he isn't. He's rich.

Are Mr. and Mrs. Golo fat?
No, they aren't. They're thin.

1. Is Peter married?
2. Is his car cheap?
3. Are Jimmy and Linda old?
4. Are New York and Tokyo small cities?

5. Is the Volkswagen a big car?
6. Is Albert thin?
7. Is his umbrella white?
8. Is Barbara tall?
9. Are you sad?

d *Make negative commands.*

Example: Listen to Dr. Pasto.
Don't listen to him.

1. Write to Mrs. Golo.
2. Read this book.
3. Look at those men.
4. Sit with Linda and me.
5. Talk to Albert.

6. Open the window.
7. Ask Maria.
8. Take these apples.
9. Wait for Peter and me.

e   *Answer the following questions as indicated.*

Examples: How much is Otis's painting? (80 dollars)

It's eighty dollars.

How old is City Park? (92 years)

It's ninety-two years old.

1. How old is Dr. Pasto? (58 years)

_____

2. How old is Barbara? (24 years)

_____

3. How old is Tino? (29 years)

_____

4. How old is the museum? (31 years)

_____

5. How much is the antique chair? (87 dollars)

_____

6. How much is the bicycle? (65 dollars)

_____

7. How much are the typewriters? (96 dollars)

_____

8. How much are the guitars? (45 dollars)

_____

9. How much are the dictionaries? (9 dollars)

_____

f   *Make questions with **who, where,** or **what** as indicated.*

Examples: The art exhibition is in City Park.   Otis is talking to Dr. Pasto.
          Where's the art exhibition?   **Who's he talking to?**

He likes fruit and vegetables.
What does he like?

1. Dr. Pasto has a butterfly collection.
2. His house is on Bunker Hill.
3. He's talking to a friend.
4. Mr. Bascomb is at the antique shop.
5. He wants an old lamp.

6. He's calling the salesman.
7. Maria is sitting with Peter.
8. They're at the movies.
9. They're watching an Italian film.

g   *Look at the picture and answer the following questions.*

1. How many dogs are there in the street?
2. How many firemen are there on the fire truck?
3. How many children are there in front of the snack bar?
4. How many policemen are there in the street?
5. How many passengers are there in Barney's taxi?
6. How many bicycles are there in front of the movie theater?
7. How many cats are there on the roof?
8. How many birds are there in the picture?
9. How many trees are there in the picture?

h   *Answer the following questions about the picture using suitable prepositions.*

Examples: Where are the dogs? _*They're in*_____ the street.

Where's the Volkswagen? _*It's between*_____ the taxi and the bus.

1. Where's the taxi? _____ the Volkswagen.

2. Where's the bus? _____ the Volkswagen.

3. Where's Mr. Bascomb? _____ the corner.

4. Where are the firemen? _____ the fire truck.

5. Where are the Japanese tourists? _____ Barney's taxi.

6. Where are the children? _____ the snack bar.

7. Where's the snack bar? _____ the street from the drugstore.

8. Where are the bicycles? _____ the movie theater.

9. Where's the pet shop? _____ the snack bar.

10. Where's the cat? _____ the roof.

i   *Answer the following questions about the picture.*

Examples: Is Mr. Bascomb crossing the street?   Is he looking at the fire truck?
          No, he isn't. He's standing at the corner.   **Yes, he is.**

1. Is he smoking?   6. Are the children eating hot dogs?
2. Is he wearing a hat?   7. Is the old woman closing the window?
3. Is Barney driving his taxi?   8. Are the dogs chasing the policeman?
4. Does he have three passengers?   9. Are the bicycles in front of the movie theater?
5. Are they Italian?   10. Is the drugstore next to the snack bar?

j   *Answer the following questions about the picture.*

Example: Where is Mr. Bascomb standing?
         He's standing at the corner.

1. What's he looking at?   7. What are the children eating?
2. Is he smoking a pipe or a cigar?   8. What are they looking at?
3. What's Barney doing?   9. What's the old woman doing?
4. What are his passengers doing?   10. Is the young woman leaving the drugstore
5. Where's the policeman standing?   or the movie theater?
6. What are the dogs chasing?

k   *Complete the following sentences as indicated.*

Example: Jimmy is in the park. He has ___*his*___ camera with ___*him*___ .

1. Barbara and Tino are at the beach. They have _____ radio with _____ .

2. Anne is at the bus stop. Does she have _____ handbag with _____ ?

3. Are you going to school? Do you have _____ notebook with _____ ?

4. Barney is at the garage. He has _____ girlfriend with _____ .

5. They're playing poker. They have _____ cards with _____ .

6. I'm going to the party. I have _____ guitar with _____ .

7. Maria is cold. She doesn't have _____ coat with _____ .

8. We're at home. We have _____ friends with _____ .

l   *Answer the following questions in the negative as indicated.*

Examples: Where's Barbara's car?   Where's the Browns' apartment?
          She doesn't have a car.   **They don't have an apartment.**

1. Where's their typewriter?   5. Where's the children's desk?
2. Where's Sam's dictionary?   6. Where's their football?
3. Where's Mrs. Golo's umbrella?   7. Where's Albert's bicycle?
4. Where's her hat?   8. Where's his guitar?

m   *Complete each one of the following sentences with a possessive adjective and a possessive pronoun.*

Example: I have ___*my*___ classes in the morning and Linda has ___*hers*___ in the afternoon.

1. They have _____ ideas and we have _____ .

2. You have _____ friends and I have _____ .

3. Linda is studying in _____ room and Jimmy is studying in _____ .

4. You have _____ birthday in July and I have _____ in August.

5. We're writing to _____ friends and they're writing to _____ .

6. He's helping _____ family and she's helping _____ .

7. You're cleaning _____ house and they're cleaning _____ .

8. Peter is washing _____ car and I'm washing _____ .

VOCABULARY

art	exhibition	many	show (v.)
August	expression	meat	snack
			store
birthday	fireman	ordinary	strange
	fire truck	original	strong
certainly	first		study (v.)
cigarette	fruit	painting	
composition		passenger	talker
cross (v.)	hot dog	personality	true
		pet	
December	idea	poker	unusual
different	include	public	
drive (v.)			vegetarian
drug	Japanese	Sagittarian	
drugstore	July	sale	when
		shape (n.)	
enjoy	lover	shop (n.)	

EXPRESSIONS

at the moment   for sale   Let's see.

TEST

1. This is Mr. Poole.
   _____ is a teacher.
   a. Him   c. He
   b. It   d. She

2. _____ book is interesting.
   a. These   c. Those
   b. There   d. This

3. _____ flowers are beautiful.
   a. Those   c. That
   b. There   d. This

4. The table is _____ the kitchen.
   a. on   c. to
   b. at   d. in

5. The umbrella is _____ the floor.
   a. at   c. in
   b. on   d. to

6. Nancy is _____ the airport.
   a. to   c. at
   b. on   d. with

7. Tino _____ thirsty.
   a. is   c. have
   b. has   d. are

8. Are _____ pretty girls?
   a. she   c. them
   b. they   d. her

9. The flowers _____ in the vase.
   a. are   c. be
   b. is   d. have

10. Tino isn't short. He's _____.
    a. poor   c. sad
    b. happy   d. tall

11. Those books aren't cheap.
    They're _____.
    a. old   c. small
    b. expensive d. rich

12. They _____ the bank.
    a. are going   c. are going to
    b. is going   d. going to

13. She _____ the menu.
    a. is looking   c. is looking to
    b. are looking   d. is looking at

14. _____ He's at the garage.
    a. Where is he?   c. Who is he?
    b. What is he?   d. How is he?

15. _____ They're fine, thank you.
    a. Who are they?   c. How are they?
    b. What are they? d. Where are they?

16. _____ is she going?
    a. What   c. Who
    b. Where   d. To where

17. _____ is he? He's Dr. Pasto.
    a. Where   c. How
    b. What   d. Who

18. Wait _____ Anne.
    a. for   c. to
    b. at   d. from

19. Who is she looking _____?
    a. on   c. to
    b. at   d. from

20. He's listening _____ the radio.
    a. at   c. of
    b. in   d. to

21. Talk _____ them.

    a. to   c. on
    b. at   d. of

22. Put these glasses _____ the table.

    a. to   c. on
    b. in   d. at

23. They don't have _____ books.

    a. there   c. theirs
    b. their   d. them

24. This magazine is _____.

    a. to her   c. hers
    b. her   d. of her

25. That desk is _____.

    a. mine   c. me
    b. my   d. to me

26. Whose apartment is that?
    It's _____.

    a. to him   c. his
    b. Mr. Jones   d. him

27. Give the flowers _____.

    a. them   c. to they
    b. their   d. to them

28. That man is hungry.
    Give _____ some food.

    a. he   c. his
    b. her   d. him

29. Mrs. Jones is in Italy.
    Write _____ a letter.

    a. to her   c. hers
    b. her   d. him

30. Do they have a car?
    No, they _____.

    a. don't   c. aren't
    b. doesn't d. have

31. _____ an apple in the kitchen.

    a. It has   c. It's
    b. There are   d. There's

32. Where are the cups?
    _____ on the shelf.

    a. They're c. There is
    b. There are   d. Their

33. What are those?
    _____ dictionaries.

    a. There are   c. They're
    b. There's some   d. It's a

34. _____ milk in the bottle.

    a. There's some   c. It's a
    b. There's a   d. There are

35. _____ letters on the desk.

    a. There's c. Their
    b. There are   d. They're

36. What time is it? _____

    a. It's hot.   c. It's two o'clock.
    b. It's ten dollars.   d. It's six years old.

37. How old is that watch? _____

    a. It's one o'clock.   c. It's expensive.
    b. It's fifty dollars.   d. It's six years old.

38. How much is that typewriter? _____

    a. It's in the office.   c. It's six years old.
    b. It's fifty dollars.   d. It's very good.

39. Jimmy _____ ice cream.

    a. have   c. likes
    b. like   d. want

40. She's thirsty.
    She _____ a glass of water.

    a. wants   c. have
    b. want   d. likes

CHAPTER EIGHT

Present simple   Adverbs of frequency

a

b

a   Barbara Sherman is a secretary
at the City Bank. She works
every day from nine to five.
She lives a long way from her job,
and she doesn't drive a car.
She always takes the bus
to work.

1. Is Barbara a teacher or a secretary?
2. What hours does she work?
3. Does she live near her job?
4. Does she drive a car?
5. How does she go to work?

b   Sam Brown lives in Wickam City.
Every morning he gets up at seven
o'clock and takes a shower. Then he
gets dressed and eats breakfast.
Sam always has bananas and apple
juice for breakfast.

1. Where does Mr. Brown live?
2. When does he get up?
3. Does he take a bath or a shower?
4. What does he do before breakfast?
5. What does he have for breakfast?

AFFIRMATIVE

Barbara works at the bank.
She_____.
Mr. Bascomb _____.
He _____.

They work every day.
You _____.
We _____.
I_____.

c   *Answer the following questions as indicated.*

Examples: Does Barbara work from nine to five?
   Yes, she works from nine to five every day.

   Do the children walk to school?
   Yes, they walk to school every day.

1. Does Peter drive to work?
2. Does Anne play the guitar?
3. Do Mr. and Mrs. Bascomb read the newspaper?
4. Does Sam eat bananas?
5. Does Mabel work in the garden?
6. Does Linda help her mother?
7. Do Barbara and Tino listen to the radio?
8. Does Tino drink coffee?
9. Does Barbara take the bus?

ANNE: Do you have a boyfriend, Barbara?

BARBARA: Yes, I do. His name's Tino.

ANNE: Tell me about him.

BARBARA: He's tall and handsome, and
            his family comes from Italy.

ANNE: Does he speak Italian?

BARBARA: Not with me. I don't understand
            a word of it.

ANNE: Does he have a good job?

BARBARA: Yes. He works for his father.

ANNE: What kind of business does his
            father have?

BARBARA: He has an Italian restaurant.

INTERROGATIVE

Does Tino speak Italian?   Do the Martinolis come from Italy?
_____ he _____?   ____ our neighbors _____?
_____ Maria _____?   ____ your friends _____?
_____ she _____?   ____ those people _____?

d   *Make questions as indicated.*

     Examples: Tino speaks Italian.   (French)
             Does he speak French, too?

             Jimmy and Linda walk to school.   (home)
             Do they walk home, too?

1. Barbara works at the bank.   (at home)
2. She lives a long way from her job.   (a long way from her boyfriend)
3. Barney drives a taxi.   (a bus)
4. Peter and Maria like Japanese food.   (Mexican food)
5. She drinks tea.   (coffee)
6. He has a sports car.   (a motorcycle)
7. Albert and Jimmy like hamburgers.   (hot dogs)
8. Albert wants some ketchup. (some mustard)
9. Dr. Pasto chases butterflies.   (dogs)

NEGATIVE

Barbara doesn't understand Italian.   They don't work at night.
She _____.   You _____.
Mr. Bascomb _____.   We _____.
He _____.   I _____.

e   *Make negative sentences as indicated.*

     Examples: Anne and Barbara don't work on Sunday.   (on Saturday)
             They don't work on Saturday, either.

             Barbara doesn't live near the bank.   (near the hospital)
             She doesn't live near the hospital, either.

1. Otis doesn't like meat.   (chicken)
2. He doesn't eat breakfast every day.   (lunch every day)
3. Mr. and Mrs. Brown don't have a big car.   (a big house)
4. They don't clean the kitchen every day.   (the bathroom every day)
5. Anne doesn't speak French.   (Spanish)
6. She doesn't know Tino.   (Barney)
7. Jimmy and Linda don't like cold weather.   (hot weather)
8. They don't go to the beach every day.   (to the park every day)
9. Mr. Bascomb doesn't understand Italian.   (German)

Otis <u>always</u> eats
fruit and vegetables.

He <u>never</u> eats meat.

Johnny <u>often</u> goes to
the movies.

He <u>seldom</u> watches television.

Mr. Bascomb <u>usually</u>
drinks coffee.

He <u>sometimes</u> drinks tea.

ADVERBS OF FREQUENCY

They always get up at six o'clock.
_____ usually _____.
_____ often _____.
_____ sometimes _____.
_____ seldom _____.
_____ never _____.

a   _Add **always, usually, often, sometimes, seldom,** or **never** to the following sentences._

Examples: Otis eats meat. (never)
Otis never eats meat.

Mr. and Mrs. Bascomb listen to classical music. (always)
Mr. and Mrs. Bascomb always listen to classical music.

1. He drinks coffee. (usually)
2. She wears expensive clothes. (often)
3. Anne and Barbara work on Sunday. (never)
4. Barbara takes the red bus. (always)
5. Anne plays the guitar. (often)
6. Barney gets up at seven o'clock. (seldom)
7. Albert and Linda study at home. (usually)
8. He plays football. (sometimes)
9. Peter walks to work. (seldom)

INTERROGATIVE

Do they always take the bus?
_____ usually _____?
_____ often _____?
_____ ever _____?

NEGATIVE

They don't always take the bus.
_____ usually _____ .
_____ often _____ .
_____ ever _____ .

b   _Add **always, usually, often,** or **ever** to the following sentences._

Examples: Does Barbara take the red bus? (always)
Does Barbara always take the red bus?

Peter and Maria don't work on Saturday. (usually)
Peter and Maria don't usually work on Saturday.

1. Does he walk to work? (ever)
2. Do Jimmy and Linda wash the dishes? (often)
3. He doesn't make breakfast in the morning. (always)
4. They don't drink tea. (usually)
5. Does Tino speak French? (ever)
6. He doesn't read the newspaper. (usually)
7. Anne and Barbara don't wear hats. (often)
8. Does Mr. Smith watch television? (always)
9. Mr. and Mrs. Brown don't go to the beach. (often)

MARTY: Good morning, Mrs. Golo.

MRS. GOLO: What time is it, Marty?

MARTY: It's half past nine.

MRS. GOLO: That's right. You're late. You're
                always late.

MARTY: The buses are often late, too, Mrs. Golo.

MRS. GOLO: Look, Susie takes the bus,
                and she's always on time.

MARTY: But she's never early. Right,
                Mrs. Golo?

MRS. GOLO: Sit down and be quiet.

ADVERBS OF FREQUENCY

She's always on time.
_____ usually _____.
_____ often _____.
_____ sometimes ____.
_____ seldom _____.
_____ never _____.

c   *Add **always, usually, often, sometimes, seldom**, or **never** to the following sentences.*

Examples: Marty is on time. (never)
          Marty is never on time.

          The buses are late. (often)
          The buses are often late.

1. Susie is on time. (always)
2. Mr. Brown is early. (sometimes)
3. Tino is happy. (usually)
4. Barney is worried. (never)
5. Paris is beautiful. (always)
6. Bankers are poor. (seldom)
7. Antique clocks are expensive. (usually)
8. Old books are interesting. (often)
9. Policemen are friendly. (sometimes)
10. Teachers are rich. (seldom)

d   *Answer the following questions about yourself.*

Example: Are you often late?
           Yes, I am. OR No, I'm never late. I'm always on time.

1. Are you always happy?
2. Are you ever sad?
3. Are you often hungry?
4. Are you often thirsty?
5. Are you usually on time?
6. Are you ever late?
7. Are your friends sometimes late?
8. Are you often in a hurry?
9. Are you ever worried?

Jack Grubb works at night. In the afternoon he goes to the park.
He usually sits on a bench and reads the newspaper. Sometimes he meets
interesting people in the park. He often talks with them about sports
and politics. He knows a lot about these subjects. Mr. Grubb doesn't have
a college education, but he's an intelligent man. He reads two or three
books a week. At the moment Mr. Grubb isn't reading or talking.
He's feeding the pigeons. He usually gives them bread crumbs.
Mr. Grubb always has a good time in the park.

a   *Answer the following questions about the story.*

1. Does Jack work during the day?
2. Where does he go in the afternoon?
3. What does he do there?
4. Does he ever meet interesting people in the park?
5. What does he often talk about?
6. Does Jack have a college education?
7. How many books does he read a week?
8. Is he talking or reading at the moment?
9. What's he doing?
10. What does he usually give the pigeons?

b   *Answer the following questions as indicated.*

Example: When does the bank open? (10:00)
    It opens at ten o'clock.

1. When does the bank close? (3:00)
2. When does the post office open? (9:00)
3. When does the post office close? (5:00)
4. When does Mr. Brown get up? (7:00)
5. When does he go to work? (7:45)
6. When do Anne and Barbara have lunch? (12:30)
7. When do they go home? (5:00)
8. When does the bus come? (5:15)
9. When does Linda have her French class? (2:00)

c   *Make negative sentences as indicated.*

Examples: Anne and Barbara work at the bank. (at the library)
    They don't work at the library.

    Barbara takes the red bus. (the green bus)
    She doesn't take the green bus.

1. She lives on Lime Street. (on Vine Street)
2. She has an apartment. (a house)
3. That house belongs to Dr. Pasto. (Mr. Grubb)
4. Mr. and Mrs. Golo live near the post office. (near the bank)
5. They listen to classical music. (pop music)
6. Mr. Bascomb smokes cigars. (cigarettes)
7. He gets up at six o'clock. (at six thirty)
8. The post office closes at five o'clock. (at five thirty)
9. They play football in the park. (at the beach)

d   *Answer the following questions, using short answers.*

Examples: Do Jimmy and Linda have a friend named Albert?
Yes, they do.

Does Albert play basketball?
No, he doesn't.

1. Do Anne and Barbara work at the library?
2. Does Barbara take the bus to work?
3. Does she speak Italian?
4. Does Tino speak Italian?
5. Does he have a job at the airport?

6. Do the Browns have a big house?
7. Do they have a garden?
8. Does Otis like meat?
9. Does he like fruit and vegetables?

e   *Complete the following sentences using suitable prepositions.*

Example: Sam always gets up ___*at*___ seven o'clock ___*in*___ the morning.

1. Barbara works _____ the bank _____ nine _____ five.

2. She lives a long way _____ the bank.

3. The drugstore is _____ the street _____ the snack bar.

4. The cat is sitting _____ the roof _____ the garage.

5. The post office closes _____ twelve o'clock _____ Saturday.

6. Mr. Grubb always goes _____ the park _____ the afternoon.

7. The Martinolis come _____ Italy.

8. I'm giving this book _____ Maria _____ her birthday.

9. The glasses are _____ the shelf _____ the kitchen.

f   *Change the following sentences as indicated.*

Example: Otis is showing some paintings <u>to Dr. Pasto</u>.
He's showing <u>him</u> some paintings.

1. Peter is taking some flowers <u>to Maria.</u>
2. Sam is giving a typewriter <u>to Jimmy and Linda.</u>
3. Barbara is showing a photograph <u>to Tino.</u>
4. We're taking some books <u>to the students.</u>
5. Linda is giving a bone <u>to the dog</u>.
6. Jimmy is writing a letter <u>to his girlfriend.</u>
7. Albert is showing his camera <u>to the Browns.</u>
8. Mrs. Golo is taking some milk <u>to the cat.</u>
9. Nancy is giving a dictionary <u>to Barney.</u>

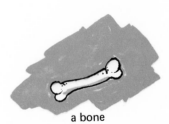

a bone

g   *Look at the pictures and answer the following questions.*

   1. Does Barney often shave?
       No, he seldom shaves.
   2. Does Mr. Bascomb often smoke cigars?
       Yes, he usually smokes cigars.
   3. Does Anne often sing in the shower?
   4. Does Jack ever cut the grass?
   5. Do Barbara and Tino ever listen to records?
   6. Does Barbara usually take the bus to work?
   7. Does Dr. Pasto often play the piano?
   8. Do Jimmy and Linda ever go to the beach?

h   *Look at the pictures and answer the following questions.*

   1. Is Barney brushing his teeth?
       No, he isn't. He's shaving.
   2. Is Mr. Bascomb smoking?
       Yes, he is.
   3. Is Anne taking a bath?
   4. Is Jack resting?
   5. Are Barbara and Tino listening to the radio?
   6. Is Barbara walking to work?
   7. Is Dr. Pasto playing the piano?
   8. Are Jimmy and Linda going to the park?

i   *Answer the following questions about yourself, using adverbs of frequency.*

   1. Do you ever get up at five o'clock?
   2. Do you often have milk for breakfast?
   3. Do you sometimes take the bus?
   4. Do you ever play cards?
   5. Do you often read the newspaper?
   6. Do your friends ever have parties?
   7. Do you often listen to the radio?
   8. Do you ever write to your friends?
   9. Do you often wash the dishes?

j   *Write a short composition about the things you do every day.*

VOCABULARY

always	early	late	pop music	subject
	education	live (v.)		
banana	either	love (v.)	quiet	understand
before	ever			usually
bench		motorcycle	record (n.)	
bone	feed			way
bread crumbs		never	Saturday	weather
	half		seldom	word
college	hamburger	often	shave (v.)	
	hurry		sometimes	
		pigeon	speak	
during	know	politics	sports car	

EXPRESSIONS OF TIME

early	on time	from nine to five
late	on Saturday	five times a week

PRONUNCIATION

s

eat<u>s</u>	hel<u>ps</u>	want<u>s</u>
drink<u>s</u>	work<u>s</u>	make<u>s</u>
smoke<u>s</u>	paint<u>s</u>	walk<u>s</u>

Otis never smokes or drinks.

He often walks to the park
and paints pictures.

z

play<u>s</u>	drive<u>s</u>	call<u>s</u>
wear<u>s</u>	clean<u>s</u>	give<u>s</u>
live<u>s</u>	read<u>s</u>	show<u>s</u>

Mrs. Bascomb seldom calls her friends.

She lives in a beautiful house and
drives a big car.

iz

watch<u>es</u>	wash<u>es</u>	cross<u>es</u>
danc<u>es</u>	brush<u>es</u>	kiss<u>es</u>
	clos<u>es</u>	

Barbara always brushes her hair
and washes her face.

She sometimes watches television.

Every morning, Mr. Brown brushes his teeth, shaves, and takes a shower.
Then he eats breakfast, reads the newspaper, and kisses his wife goodbye.

PRESENT SIMPLE Affirmative

He She	lives	
I You We They	live	in New York.

Negative

He She	doesn't (does not)	
I You We They	don't (do not)	live in New York.

Interrogative

Does	he she	
Do	I you we they	live in New York?

Short Answers

Yes,	he she	does.
	I you we they	do.

No,	he she	doesn't.
	I you we they	don't.

Question with WHAT, WHEN, WHERE, WHO

Sam wears a white hat.	What does he wear?	A white hat.
He gets up at seven o'clock.	When does he get up?	At seven o'clock.
Barbara works at the bank.	Where does she work?	At the bank.
She likes Tino Martinoli.	Who does she like?	Tino Martinoli.

ADVERBS OF FREQUENCY

They	always usually often sometimes seldom never	come	early. late. on time.

They're	always usually often sometimes seldom never	early. late. on time.

Interrogative

Do they	ever	take the bus?

Negative

They	never	take the bus.

CHAPTER NINE

Present simple vs. present continuous

Other/another
Some/any

a Jimmy Brown is a student in high school. He likes his classes and gets good grades. Jimmy usually studies with his friends in the school library. He often helps them with their lessons. After school they sometimes go to the park and play football. Right now Jimmy is watching television.

1. Where does Jimmy study?
2. Is he studying now?
3. Does Jimmy help his friends with their lessons?
4. Is he helping them now?
5. Where does Jimmy go after school?
6. Is he going there now?
7. What's he doing?

b Tino Martinoli works every day at his father's restaurant. He's very friendly and smiles at all the customers. Tino's friends often come and see him at the restaurant. They usually talk about sports. At the moment Tino is playing tennis with Barbara and he's losing.

1. What does Tino do every day?
2. Is he working now?
3. What does Tino talk about with his friends?
4. Is he talking with them now?
5. What's he doing?
6. Is he smiling?
7. Why not?

PRESENT SIMPLE

He often goes to the park.
————— plays football.
————— reads a book.
————— watches TV.

PRESENT CONTINUOUS

Is he going to the park now?
—— playing football ——?
—— reading a book——?
—— watching TV ———?

c *Make questions using the present continuous.*

Examples: Jimmy often helps his friends.
Is he helping them now?

They usually talk about sports.
Are they talking about sports now?

1. They sometimes go to the park.
2. Dr. Pasto sometimes works in the garden.
3. He usually chases butterflies.
4. Barbara and Tino often play tennis.
5. She sometimes listens to records.
6. He usually reads the newspaper.
7. Jimmy and Linda often make breakfast.
8. They usually wash the dishes.
9. They sometimes clean the kitchen.

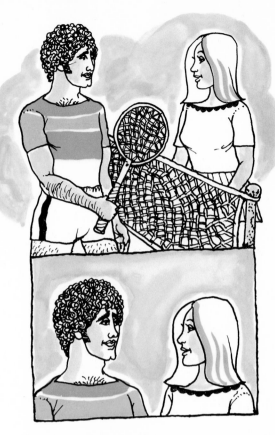

TINO: You're playing well today, Barbara.

BARBARA: I always play well, Tino.

TINO: But you don't always win.

BARBARA: I'm winning today.

TINO: You're just lucky.

BARBARA: That's right, Tino. I'm lucky today.

MABEL: Are you enjoying your dinner, Sam?

SAM: Of course. I always enjoy my dinner.

MABEL: But you never tell me it's good.

SAM: I'm telling you now, it's fantastic.

PRESENT SIMPLE

Do they always go to the park?
_____ take sandwiches?
_____ play tennis?
_____ walk home?

PRESENT CONTINUOUS

They're going to the park today.
_____ taking sandwiches _____.
_____ playing tennis _____.
_____ walking home _____.

d   *Answer the following questions as indicated.*

Examples: Do Barbara and Tino always play tennis?
No, but they're playing tennis today.

Does Barbara always win?
No, but she's winning today.

1. Does Sam always cut the grass?
2. Does Nancy always take the bus?
3. Do Jimmy and Linda always clean the house?
4. Does she always wear jeans?
5. Do Peter and Maria always go to the beach?
6. Do they always have hot dogs?
7. Does Mr. Bascomb always work in the garden?
8. Does Anne always go to the movies?
9. Does Otis always work at home?

jeans

PRESENT CONTINUOUS

She's reading the newspaper.
_____ making breakfast.
_____ drinking orange juice.
_____ taking a shower.

PRESENT SIMPLE

She reads the newspaper every morning.
____ makes breakfast _____ .
____ drinks orange juice _____ .
____ takes a shower _____ .

e   *Change the following sentences as indicated.*

Examples: Albert is watching television. (every day)
He watches television every day.

Mr. and Mrs. Golo are going to the movies. (every week)
They go to the movies every week.

1. Dr. Pasto is chasing butterflies. (every afternoon)
2. Anne's taking a shower. (every morning)
3. Jimmy and Linda are washing the dishes. (every day)
4. Sam is cutting the grass. (every month)
5. Johnnie is painting the house. (every year)
6. Nick and Barney are playing cards. (every Saturday)
7. Nancy is cleaning the windows. (every week)
8. Peter is shaving. (every morning)
9. Jack is watching the football game. (every Sunday)

Another rainy day.

MR. BASCOMB: Goodbye, dear.

MRS. BASCOMB: Take your umbrella, John. It's raining.

MR. BASCOMB: Do we have another umbrella?

MRS. BASCOMB: Yes, it's in the closet.

MR. BASCOMB: Please get it for me.

MRS. BASCOMB: Here's the other umbrella.

MR. BASCOMB: Thank you very much, dear.

ANOTHER

There's another umbrella in the closet.
_____ coat _____.
_____ hat _____.
_____ tie _____.

a   *Make sentences using **another**.*

   Examples: There's a magazine on the table. (on the chair)
              There's another magazine on the chair.

              Barbara has a vase in her kitchen. (in her living room)
              She has another vase in her living room.

   1. Mr. Bascomb has a clock in his office. (in his bedroom)
   2. Peter has a radio in his car. (in his office)
   3. There's a library on Main Street. (on Lime Street)
   4. There's a bottle on the shelf. (on the floor)
   5. Nancy has a mirror in her bathroom. (in her bedroom)
   6. She has a pen in her pocket. (in her desk)
   7. There's a bus stop at the post office. (at the bank)
   8. There's a notebook on the table. (in the desk)
   9. There's a cat in the tree. (on the roof)

THE OTHER

He wants the other umbrella.
_____ coat.
_____ hat.
_____ tie.

b   *Make sentences using **one** and **the other**.*

   Examples: There are two dictionaries in the bookcase. (Spanish/French)
              One is Spanish and the other is French.

              We have two lamps. (yellow/green)
              One is yellow and the other is green.

   1. Albert has two radios. (cheap/expensive)
   2. Barbara has two hats. (new/old)
   3. Sam has two brothers. (tall/short)
   4. Nancy has two cats. (black/white)
   5. There are two roses in the vase. (red/yellow)
   6. There are two girls at the bus stop. (fat/thin)
   7. There are two letters on the table. (from England/from France)
   8. There are two libraries in the city. (on Main Street/on Lime Street)
   9. There are two houses on Bunker Hill. (modern/traditional)

Peter has <u>some</u> cigarettes.

But he doesn't have <u>any</u> matches.

Maria has <u>some</u> milk.

But she doesn't have <u>any</u> sugar.

Mrs. Bascomb has <u>some</u> bread.

But she doesn't have <u>any</u> butter.

Jack has <u>some</u> bills.

But he doesn't have <u>any</u> money.

STOREKEEPER: Do you want any help, ma'am?

MABEL BROWN: Yes. I'm looking for some bananas.

STOREKEEPER: I'm sorry. There aren't any bananas left.

MABEL BROWN: Oh, that's a shame!

c *Make statements about the fruit in the boxes using* **some** *or* **any**.

Examples: apples
          There are some apples.

          bananas
          There aren't any bananas.

1. pears
2. peaches
3. pineapples
4. cherries
5. oranges
6. grapes
7. lemons

Barney Field works for the Speedy Cab Company. He's an excellent
driver and knows the city well. Barney enjoys his work because he meets
interesting people on the job. He's very friendly and always talks with his
passengers. Sometimes he tells them amusing stories about his experiences
as a taxi driver. Barney often meets foreign visitors, and he gives them
useful information about the city. He knows all the good restaurants,
hotels, and nightclubs.

Barney takes good care of his car. He stops at Nick's Garage every day,
but he seldom buys any gas there. It's very hot this afternoon, and Nick is
putting water in the radiator. One of his employees is cleaning the windows
and the other is putting air in the tires. Barney is drinking a cup of coffee
and having a short conversation with Nick.

"My garage is a long way from the center of town," says Nick. "Why do
you always bring your car here?"

"Because you're my friend," says Barney. "And I never forget my friends."

a   *Answer the following questions about the story.*

    1. What company does Barney work for?
    2. Why does Barney enjoy his work?
    3. Does Barney often talk with his passengers?
    4. What does he tell them?
    5. Where does Barney go every day?
    6. Does he often buy gas there?
    7. What's Nick doing at this moment?
    8. What are his employees doing?
    9. What's Barney doing?
  10. Is Nick's Garage near the center of town?
  11. Why does Barney always take his car there?

b   *Answer the following questions using adverbs of frequency.*

    Examples: Does Barney often talk with his passengers? (yes/always)
        Yes, he always talks with his passengers.

          Do Anne and Barbara drive to work? (no/never)
        No, they never drive to work.

    1. Does Barbara play tennis? (yes/often)
    2. Does Jimmy study at home? (yes/sometimes)
    3. Do Mr. and Mrs. Brown often watch television? (no/seldom)
    4. Do they listen to the radio? (yes/usually)
    5. Does Albert ever play basketball? (no/never)
    6. Do Nick and Barney read the newspaper? (yes/often)
    7. Does Jimmy help his friends? (yes/always)
    8. Do Mr. and Mrs. Golo work in the garden? (yes/sometimes)
    9. Does Jack ever get up at seven o'clock? (no/never)

c   *Combine the following sentences as indicated.*

    Example: Barney enjoys his work. It's interesting.
        Barney enjoys his work because it's interesting.

    1. He's thirsty. It's hot today.
    2. Mabel is cleaning the kitchen. It's dirty.
    3. People like Dr. Pasto. He's friendly.
    4. Mr. Bascomb is taking his umbrella. It's raining.
    5. Maria is smiling. She's happy.
    6. Otis doesn't eat meat. He's a vegetarian.
    7. Linda isn't eating her dinner. She isn't hungry.
    8. Barbara takes the bus to work. She doesn't have a car.
    9. Peter isn't working today. He's sick.

d   *Make negative sentences as indicated.*

Example: Peter has some cigarettes. (matches)
   But he doesn't have any matches.

1. Linda has some envelopes. (stamps)
2. Mrs. Golo has some glasses. (cups)
3. Peter has some coffee. (tea)
4. Albert has some mustard. (mayonnaise)
5. Anne has some fruit. (vegetables)
6. Jack has some bills. (money)
7. There are some potatoes. (tomatoes)
8. There's some ice cream. (cake)
9. There are some apples. (bananas)

e   *Change the following sentences using object pronouns.*

Example: She's getting the umbrella for her husband.
   She's getting it for him.

1. He's showing his paintings to Dr. Pasto.
2. I'm taking these oranges to Maria.
3. She's getting the magazines for Linda and me.
4. He's giving the typewriter to the students.
5. We're buying the radio for Anne.
6. She's bringing the letters to Mr. Bascomb.
7. He's buying the statue for Tino and me.
8. I'm giving that clock to my friends.
9. We're taking this lamp to Mrs. Golo.

f   *Write a short composition about your school or your job.*

VOCABULARY

air	conversation	gas	lemon	pineapple	tell
amusing	customer	grade (n.)	lose (v.)		tennis
another		grape	lucky	radiator	tie (n.)
	driver			rainy	tire (v.)
because		high	money		town
	employee	hotel		shame	
care (n.)	experience		nightclub	stop	useful
center		information		storekeeper	
closet	fantastic		other	story	well (adv.)
company	foreign	jeans		sugar	win (v.)
	forget (v.)	just	peach		

EXPRESSIONS

You're just lucky.   center of town   Take good care of your car.

Thank you very much.   on the job   There aren't any left.

                       That's a shame.

PRONUNCIATION

o				**a**		
only	coat	those		clock	stop	coffee
open	cold	show		often	pot	doctor
rose	phone	smoke		hot	shop	across
home	know	window		dog	closet	modern

Don't open those envelopes.   Tom often stops at the coffee shop.
The yellow roses are by the window.   He eats a lot of hot dogs.

         The post office opens at nine o'clock.
         Joe wants a cold bottle of Coke.

SOME/ANY Affirmative

She has They have	some	apples. oranges. bread. butter.

Negative

She doesn't have They don't have	any	apples. oranges. bread. butter.

Interrogative

Does she have Do they have	any	apples? oranges? bread? butter?

Short Answers

Yes,	she does. they do.

No,	she doesn't. they don't.

There's a	lamp clock vase table	in the living room.

ANOTHER

There's another	lamp clock vase table	in the bedroom.

There are two	lamps. clocks. vases. tables.

ONE　　THE OTHER

One	lamp clock vase table	is old and the other	(lamp) (clock) (vase) (table)	is new.

PRESENT SIMPLE

He	always usually often sometimes seldom	goes to the movies.

PRESENT CONTINUOUS

Is he going to the movies now?

CHAPTER TEN

"To need"   Some/any/one
Can   as pronouns

a

b

a Peter is worried. He's a long way from the city and the gas tank is empty. He needs some gas. He's looking for a gas station, but there aren't any nearby.

1. Why is Peter worried?
2. What does he need?
3. What about oil?
4. What's Peter looking for?
5. Are there any gas stations nearby?

b Anne is coming from the shower. Her hair is wet and she's holding a towel around her. Anne doesn't have many clothes; she always wears the same dress. She needs a new one. She also needs a new pair of shoes.

1. Where's Anne coming from?
2. Is her hair wet or dry?
3. What's she holding around her?
4. Does Anne have many clothes?
5. What does she need?

AFFIRMATIVE

Anne needs some shoes.
She _____.
Jack _____.
He _____.

The children need some clothes.
We _____ .
You _____ .
I _____ .

c *Look at the pictures below and answer the following questions.*

1. What does Barney need?
   He needs some socks.
2. What does Mrs. Golo need?
3. What does Mr. Bascomb need?
4. What does Maria need?

5. What does Barbara need?
6. What does Tino need?
7. What does Mrs. Bascomb need?
8. What does Jack need?

STOREKEEPER: What do you need today, Mrs. Brown?

MRS. BROWN: I need some potatoes and tomatoes.

STOREKEEPER: Do you need any onions?

MRS. BROWN: No, I already have some,
                thank you.

MR. BASCOMB: What's the matter, sonny?

BOBBY: I don't have any money.

MR. BASCOMB: How much do you need?

BOBBY: I need two dollars.

MR. BASCOMB: Here. Take this.

BOBBY: Thank you, mister.

INTERROGATIVE

Does Mrs. Brown need any onions?   Do you need any vegetables?
_____ she _____ ?   __ they_____?
_____ Barney _____ ?   __ we _____?
_____ he _____ ?   __ the Golos _____?

d   *Make questions as indicated.*

     Example: Peter doesn't need any oil.   (gas)
                Does he need any gas?

    1.   Nancy doesn't need any milk.   (bread)
    2.   She doesn't need any coffee.   (tea)
    3.   The Browns don't need any shampoo.   (toothpaste)
    4.   They don't need any glasses.   (cups)
    5.   Anne doesn't need any stamps.   (envelopes)
    6.   She doesn't need any pencils.   (paper)
    7.   The students don't need any desks.   (chairs)
    8.   Otis doesn't need any fruit.   (vegetables)
    9.   He doesn't need any eggs.   (butter)

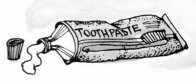

toothpaste

NEGATIVE

Mrs. Brown doesn't need any onions.   I don't need any vegetables.
She_____ .   They _____ .
Barney _____ .   We _____ .
He _____ .   The Golos _____ .

e   *Make negative sentences as indicated.*

     Example: Otis/fruit _____*Otis doesn't need any fruit.*_____

    1. He/mayonnaise _____

    2. They/milk _____

    3. You/toothpaste _____

    4. We/shampoo _____

    5. Peter/cigarettes _____

    6. I/envelopes _____

    7. She/books _____

    8. They/money _____

    9. You/clothes _____

1   Mrs. Brown is a good cook.

She can make spaghetti.
_____ chocolate cake.
_____ banana bread.
_____ fried chicken.

2   Mr. Brown has a big appetite.

He can eat a whole chicken.
_____ a chocolate cake.
_____ three hamburgers.
_____ five hot dogs.

3   Jimmy is a fine athlete.

He can play basketball.
_____ football.
_____ baseball.
_____ tennis.

4   Nancy is very intelligent.

She can speak French.
_____ German.
_____ Spanish.
_____ English.

AFFIRMATIVE

Jimmy can play tennis.
He _____ .
Linda _____ .
She _____ .

They can play the piano.
You _____ .
We _____ .
I _____ .

a   *Answer the following questions about yourself.*

1. What languages can you speak?
2. What languages can your parents speak?
3. What sports can you play?
4. What musical instruments can you play?
5. What songs can you sing?
6. What dances can you do?
7. What games can you play?
8. What dishes can you make?
9. How many eggs can you eat?

TINO: What kind of movies do you like, Barbara?

BARBARA: I like French movies.

TINO: Can you speak French?

BARBARA: No, but I can understand it.

SAM BROWN: Can you make a banana cake
                   today?

MABEL BROWN: No, I can't.

SAM BROWN: Why not?

MABEL BROWN: I don't have any bananas.

INTERROGATIVE

Can Barbara speak French?
___ the Browns _____ ?
___ Jack _____ ?
___ you _____ ?

b   *Make questions as indicated.*

Example: Tino can speak Italian.   (French)
Can he speak French, too?

1. Mr. Bascomb can play the piano.   (the violin)
2. Jack can drive a truck.   (a bus)
3. Barbara can do the tango.   (the samba)
4. Jimmy can play football.   (baseball)
5. Anne can write poetry.   (stories)
6. Mrs. Brown can make spaghetti.   (pizza)
7. Otis can paint fruit and vegetables.   (animals)
8. Sam can eat a whole chicken.   (a whole pineapple)
9. Nick can repair Italian cars.   (German cars)

a violin

A POEM
ROSES ARE RED,
VIOLETS ARE BLUE,
SUGAR IS SWEET,
AND YOU ARE, TOO.

poetry

Nick

NEGATIVE

She can't speak French.
They _____ .
He _____ .
I _____ .

c   *Make sentences as indicated.*

Example: Anne can play the guitar.   (the violin)
But she can't play the violin.

1. She can write in Spanish.   (in German)
2. Albert can play football.   (basketball)
3. Maria can ride a bicycle.   (a motorcycle)
4. I can eat a whole pineapple.   (a whole cake)
5. He can repair European cars.   (Japanese cars)
6. They can do the samba.   (the tango)
7. We can understand Italian.   (Portuguese)
8. She can make chocolate cake.   (chocolate ice cream)
9. Mr. Bascomb can drive a car.   (a bus)

Maria

a motorcycle

It's Wednesday night at the Martinoli Restaurant. Tino is taking orders from Mr. and Mrs. Hamby. They're regular customers at the restaurant. Mr. Hamby wants a big plate of spaghetti with meat sauce. For dessert he wants some Italian ice cream. His wife can't have spaghetti or ice cream. She's watching her weight. Mrs. Hamby is ordering a bowl of vegetable soup for dinner. She doesn't want any dessert.

"There's no vegetable soup," says Tino. "But I can bring you some chicken soup."

"Wonderful," says Mrs. Hamby. "I love chicken soup."

"This is a fine restaurant," says Mr. Hamby. "Except for one thing."

"What's that?" says Tino.

"There's no music."

"You need some Italian music," says Mrs. Hamby. "And some pictures of Italy on the wall."

"That's a good idea," says Tino. "I have some pictures of Venice at home. I can use them."

"Wonderful," says Mrs. Hamby. "I love Venice."

a   *Answer the following questions about the story.*

1. What night is it?
2. What's Tino doing?
3. Do Mr. and Mrs. Hamby often go to the Martinoli Restaurant?
4. What does Mr. Hamby want for dinner?
5. What does Mrs. Hamby want?
6. Does she want any dessert?
7. Why not?
8. What kind of soup does Tino have?
9. What does the restaurant need?

b   *Change the following sentences as indicated.*

Examples: There isn't any vegetable soup.   We don't have any clean glasses.
          There's no vegetable soup.   **We have no clean glasses.**

1. There aren't any green vegetables.
2. There isn't any fruit.
3. We don't have any bananas.
4. We don't have any milk.
5. There isn't any bread.
6. There aren't any eggs.
7. We don't have any coffee.
8. We don't have any clean cups.
9. There isn't any sugar.

c   *Make questions as indicated.*

Examples: they/food   *Do they need any food?*

           she/coffeepot   *Does she need a coffeepot?*

1. you/stamps _____

2. she/typewriter _____

3. Jimmy/books _____

4. your friends/money _____

5. Nancy/mirror _____

6. we/toothpaste _____

7. they/lamp _____

8. he/desk _____

9. you/matches _____

d *Make negative sentences as indicated.*

Example: Albert has a record player.
He doesn't need another one.

1. Linda has a watch.
2. The students have a library.
3. Dr. Pasto has an umbrella.
4. He has a lamp.
5. The Browns have a television.

6. They have a dictionary.
7. Barbara has a boyfriend.
8. He has a car.
9. Wickam City has an airport.

e *Answer the following questions using the short answer form.*

Example: Can you speak German?
Yes, I can. OR **No, I can't.**

1. Can you understand Russian?
2. Can you type?
3. Can you write poetry?
4. Can you drive a car?
5. Can you make pizza?

6. Can you do the samba?
7. Can you swim?
8. Can you play the piano?
9. Can you play basketball?
10. Can you eat a whole pineapple?

f *Make questions as indicated.*

Example: Barbara/French
Can Barbara speak French?

1. Mrs. Golo/spaghetti
2. Albert/a whole cake
3. Linda/the guitar
4. Mr. Bascomb/a truck
5. Maria/the tango

6. Dr. Pasto/the piano
7. Anne/poetry
8. Tino/tennis
9. Nancy/Japanese

g *Write a short composition about your best friend. What is he or she like? What kind of things can he or she do?*

VOCABULARY

already	dry	need (v.)	samba	towel
animal			same	type (v.)
appetite	empty	oil	sauce	
athlete	except	onion	shampoo	use (v.)
		order (v.)	socks	
baseball	hold (v.)		song	violin
		pair	sonny	
can (v.)	language	parent	swim	Wednesday
clothes		poetry		weight
cook (n.)	matter		tango	wet
		regular	tank	
dessert	nearby	repair (v.)	toothpaste	

EXPRESSIONS

What's the matter?

PRONUNCIATION

eyr				**er**		
hair	pear	very		her	modern	work
wear	chair	airport		skirt	dirty	dinner
care	where	repair		under	word	after
there	their	dictionary		counter	dancer	learn

Where's their dictionary?
There's a pear on the chair.

Her hamburger is on the counter.
The singer and dancer want dessert after dinner.

Mary is wearing a dirty skirt.
Their university is very modern.

NEED   Affirmative

He She	needs	some	pencils.
I You We They	need		paper.

Negative

He She	doesn't need	any	pencils.
I You We They	don't need		paper.

Interrogative

Does	he she	need any	pencils?
Do	I you we they		paper?

Short Answers

Yes,	he she	does.
	I you we they	do.

No,	he she	doesn't.
	I you we they	don't.

CAN   Affirmative

He She I You We They	can	swim.

Negative

He She I You We They	can't (cannot)	swim.

Interrogative

Can	he she I you we they	swim?

Short Answers

Yes,	he she I you we they	can.

No,	he she I you we they	can't.

NOT ANY/NO

There aren't any cookies in the jar.

They don't have any money.

There are	no	cookies in the jar.
They have	no	money.

PRONOUNS

Linda needs some envelopes.

Jimmy doesn't have any toothpaste.

I need a dictionary.

She doesn't have	any.
He needs	some.
I don't have	one.

CHAPTER ELEVEN

Simple past: **Tag questions**
"to be"   **Ordinal numbers**

TODAY

YESTERDAY

WEATHER REPORT

Today   *Yesterday*

Moscow _____ sunny.   Moscow _____ rainy.
Paris_____ sunny.   Paris_____ cold.
Rome_____ sunny.   Rome_____ windy.
London _____ sunny.   London _____ cloudy.

Today all of Europe is having good weather.
But yesterday it was rainy in Moscow.
            _____ cold in Paris.
            _____ windy in Rome.
            _____ cloudy in London.

a Nancy Paine often travels to Europe.
Yesterday she was in Moscow. She was
unhappy because the weather was bad.
It was rainy. Today Nancy is in London.
The weather is good. It's sunny. Nancy
is very happy.

1. Where was Nancy yesterday?
2. Why was she unhappy?
3. Where is Nancy today?
4. What's the weather like?

b Mr. and Mrs. Golo are on vacation in
Europe. Yesterday they were in Paris
and the weather was terrible. It was
very cold and damp. But today they're
in Rome and the weather is fantastic.
It's sunny and warm.

1. Where were Mr. and Mrs. Golo yesterday?
2. What was the weather like?
3. Where are Mr. and Mrs. Golo today?
4. What's the weather like?

Peter is returning from a trip to Spain. Johnnie Wilson is meeting him at the airport.

JOHNNIE: How was your trip, Peter?

PETER: It was wonderful.

JOHNNIE: Were the people friendly?

PETER: Yes, they were very friendly.

JOHNNIE: What was the weather like?

PETER: It wasn't very good. There was
            a lot of rain.

JOHNNIE: What were the hotels like?

PETER: Very nice. Everything was good
            except the weather.

AFFIRMATIVE

Jimmy was in the park yesterday.
He _____ .
Linda _____ .
I _____ .

They were at the movies last Friday.
You _____ .
We _____ .
The students _____ .

c *Answer the following questions as indicated.*

Example: Where was Peter last week? (in Spain)
He was in Spain.

1. Where was he last month? (in Mexico)
2. Where was Nancy last month? (in Japan)
3. Where was she last September? (in Argentina)
4. Where were Mr. and Mrs. Hamby last night? (at the Martinoli Restaurant)
5. Where were they last Sunday? (at the park)
6. Where was the President yesterday? (in London)
7. Where was he last weekend? (in Paris)
8. Where were the Browns yesterday afternoon? (at the beach)
9. Where were they last night? (at home)

NEGATIVE

Jimmy wasn't at home yesterday.
He _____ .
Linda _____ .
I _____ .

They weren't in class last Friday.
You _____ .
We _____ .
The students _____ .

d *Answer the following questions in the negative as indicated.*

Example: Where were the students last Friday? (in class)
I don't know. They weren't in class.

1. Where were your friends last weekend? (at home)
2. Where was Maria yesterday? (at the hospital)
3. Where was she last night? (at her apartment)
4. Where were Anne and Barbara last Monday? (at the office)
5. Where was Nick yesterday? (at the garage)
6. Where were the children yesterday afternoon? (at school)
7. Where was Mr. Bascomb last Wednesday? (at the bank)
8. Where were Barbara and Tino last Sunday? (at the park)
9. Where was Tino yesterday? (at the restaurant)

BARBARA: Where were you yesterday?

TINO: I was at the beach.

BARBARA: Were you with anyone?

TINO: Yes, I was with a friend named Gina.

BARBARA: Was she young and beautiful?

TINO: No, she wasn't. She was old and ugly.

BARBARA: Are you telling me the truth, Tino?

TINO: Yes, of course.

INTERROGATIVE

Was Tino at the beach yesterday?   Were you at the park last week?
____ he _____?   ____ they_____?
____ Barbara _____?   ____ we _____?
____ she_____?   ____ the Browns _____?

e   *Complete the questions using **was** and **were**.*

   Examples: ____*Was*____ Tino at the beach yesterday?

             ____*Were*____ you at home last weekend?

1. _____ Peter at the airport last week?

2. _____ he at the office this morning?

3. _____ the Browns at the park last Saturday?

4. _____ they at home yesterday afternoon?

5. _____ Anne at the museum last weekend?

6. _____ she at the bank yesterday morning?

7. _____ your friends at the hotel last night?

8. _____ they at the beach last weekend?

9. _____ Albert at the movies yesterday?

THE FOUR SEASONS

summer

fall

winter

spring

MONTHS OF THE YEAR

January	April	July	October
February	May	August	November
March	June	September	December

DAYS OF THE WEEK

Monday   Tuesday   Wednesday   Thursday   Friday   Saturday   Sunday

ORDINAL NUMBERS

1st	first	16th	sixteenth
2nd	second	17th	seventeenth
3rd	third	18th	eighteenth
4th	fourth	19th	nineteenth
5th	fifth	20th	twentieth
6th	sixth	21st	twenty-first
7th	seventh	22nd	twenty-second
8th	eighth	23rd	twenty-third
9th	ninth	24th	twenty-fourth
10th	tenth	25th	twenty-fifth
11th	eleventh	26th	twenty-sixth
12th	twelfth	27th	twenty-seventh
13th	thirteenth	28th	twenty-eighth
14th	fourteenth	29th	twenty-ninth
15th	fifteenth	30th	thirtieth

Dr. Pasto was in South America last March. Here is his travel itinerary.

MARCH						
Sunday	Monday	Tuesday	Wednesday	Thursday	Friday	Saturday
			1 *Bogotá*	2	3	4 *Quito*
5	6	7 *Lima*	8	9 *La Paz*	10	11
12 *Santiago*	13	14	15 *Buenos Aires*	16	17	18 *São Paulo*
19	20 *Rio de Janeiro*	21	22	23 *Brasília*	24	25
26 *Caracas*	27	28 *Panama City*	29	30	31	

a   *Look at the calendar and answer the following questions about Dr. Pasto's trip.*

Example: When was Dr. Pasto in Bogotá?
           He was in Bogotá on March first, second, and third.

1. When was he in Quito?
2. When was he in Lima?
3. When was he in La Paz?
4. When was he in Santiago?
5. When was he in Buenos Aires?
6. When was he in São Paulo?
7. When was he in Rio de Janeiro?
8. When was he in Brasília?
9. When was he in Caracas?
10. When was he in Panama City?

SANDY: Hi, Peter. It's a beautiful day, isn't it?

PETER: Yes, it is.

SANDY: You're going to the beach, aren't you?

PETER: Yes, I am.

SANDY: You weren't at the beach yesterday, were you?

PETER: No, I wasn't.

SANDY: You always go by car, don't you?

PETER: Yes, I do.

SANDY: I can't go with you, can I?

PETER: Yes, you can. Get in.

TAG QUESTIONS

You're going to the beach, aren't you?
They're _____, _____ they?
She's _____, isn't she?
He's _____, ____ he?

b   *Add tag questions to the following sentences.*

Examples: He always goes by car.   They were at the office yesterday.
          He always goes by car, doesn't he?   **They were at the office yesterday, weren't they?**

1. They often take the bus.
2. She's a doctor.
3. He can play tennis.
4. You're going to the market.
5. We have their address.
6. They work at the bank.
7. She was at the movies last night.
8. We're good dancers.
9. You like sports.

TAG QUESTIONS

You weren't at the beach yesterday, were you?
They_____ , ____ they?
She wasn't _____ , was she?
He _____ , ____ he?

c   *Add tag questions to the following sentences.*

Examples: I can't go with you.   He doesn't have a telephone.
          I can't go with you, can I?   **He doesn't have a telephone, does he?**

1. They aren't at home.
2. The bank wasn't open yesterday.
3. You don't have a dictionary.
4. He isn't taking the bus.
5. I don't know her.
6. You aren't a teacher.
7. She doesn't want another job.
8. They weren't at the party.
9. He can't swim.

It's Tuesday morning, June 25. Mr. Bascomb is at the bank. He's talking with some businessmen from Chicago. They're representatives of a large toy company. Mr. Bascomb and his guests are discussing plans for the construction of a toy factory in Wickam City. Mr. Bascomb thinks it's a good idea. He always encourages the establishment of new businesses in his city.

"It's good for the economy," says Mr. Bascomb. "New businesses provide more jobs for the people and money for the city."

Mr. Bascomb works long hours and seldom takes a vacation. It's very unusual when he doesn't come to work. Yesterday was an unusual day. Mr. Bascomb wasn't at work. He was at home. He was sick in bed all day. But he wasn't alone. His wife and his dog were there with him.

a   *Answer the following questions about the story.*

    1. What day is it?
    2. Where is Mr. Bascomb?
    3. Who is he talking with?
    4. What kind of company do they represent?
    5. What are they discussing?
    6. Why does Mr. Bascomb encourage new businesses?
    7. How often does Mr. Bascomb take a vacation?
    8. Was he at work yesterday?
    9. Was he sick?
  10. Was he alone?

b   *Make questions with* **what . . . like.**

    Examples: weather/London
                What was the weather like in London?

                 hotels/Spain
                What were the hotels like in Spain?

    1. restaurants/Rome
    2. beer/Germany
    3. cafes/France
    4. parks/England
    5. music/Brazil
    6. museums/Paris
    7. people/Mexico City
    8. food/Moscow
    9. transportation/Japan

c   *Give short answers to the following questions.*

    Example: You have a bicycle, don't you?
              Yes, I do. OR **No, I don't.**

    1. You like classical music, don't you?
    2. You're a good dancer, aren't you?
    3. You can play the guitar, can't you?
    4. You're at home every night, aren't you?
    5. You don't speak Russian, do you?
    6. You aren't thinking about the weekend, are you?
    7. You weren't at the park last Sunday, were you?
    8. You can't drive a car, can you?
    9. You don't have a watch, do you?

d   *Write a short composition about your favorite season. Why is it special?*

VOCABULARY

alone	encourage	June	provide	sunny	vacation
anyone	establishment				
April		last (adj.)	rain (n.)	tenth	warm
	factory	lot	report (n.)	terrible	was
beer	fall (n.)		represent	third	weekend
	February	March	representative	thirteenth	were
calendar	fifteenth	market	return (v.)	thirtieth	windy
cloudy	fifth	May		Thursday	winter
construction	fourteenth		second	toy	
	fourth	nineteenth	September	travel (v.)	yesterday
damp	Friday	ninth	seventeenth	trip	
discuss		November	seventh	truth	
	guest		sick	Tuesday	
economy		October	sixteenth	twelfth	
eighteenth	itinerary		sixth	twentieth	
eighth		plan (n.)	spring		
eleventh	January	president	summer	unhappy	

EXPRESSIONS

go by car   get in   sick in bed

Past Time Expressions

yesterday	last night	last weekend
yesterday morning	last Friday	last month
yesterday afternoon	last week	last year

PRONUNCIATION

a				ae		
sock	often	economy		can	sandwich	bank
shop	pocket	politics		hat	dancer	stamp
job	across	doctor		black	glass	plant
box	bottle	coffee		apple	Spanish	shampoo

The doctor often walks to his office.
Tom wants some hot coffee.

Sam can understand Spanish.
Nancy is asking for a glass of apple juice.

Dottie has a lot of black socks.
Dan is washing the pots and pans.

Past of TO BE   Affirmative

He She I	was	
You We They	were	in Paris yesterday.

Negative

He She I	wasn't (was not)	
You We They	weren't (were not)	in Paris yesterday.

Interrogative

Was	he she I	
Were	you we they	in Paris yesterday?

Short Answers

Yes,	he she I	was.
	you we they	were.

No,	he she I	wasn't.
	you we they	weren't.

TAG QUESTIONS

It's a beautiful day,	isn't it?
They're going to the beach,	aren't they?
You have an umbrella,	don't you?
She was at the movies,	wasn't she?
He can play the piano,	can't he?
He likes music,	doesn't he?

There aren't any matches,	are there?
He isn't working today,	is he?
They don't like football,	do they?
You weren't at the party,	were you?
She can't drive a truck,	can she?
He doesn't have a telephone,	does he?

CHAPTER TWELVE

12

Simple past:
   affirmative

Simple past:
   negative and
   interrogative

Yesterday . . .

1

Otis walked to the park.

2

He watched a basketball game.

3

He played chess.

4

He listened to some musicians.

Last night . . .

5

The movie started at seven o'clock.

6

It ended at nine o'clock.

Last Sunday . . .

1

Anne sang for Barbara and Tino.

2

Dr. Pasto found an African butterfly.

3

Nancy bought a motorcycle.

4

Linda made a birdhouse.

5

Peter drove to the beach.

6

He took his dog with him.

7

They swam in the ocean.

8

Peter lost his car keys.

SIMPLE PAST TENSE OF REGULAR VERBS

She worked in the garden.
___ washed the car.
___ cleaned the kitchen.
___ prepared dinner.
___ rested after dinner.

a   *Complete the following sentences using the simple past tense.*

Example: They (walk) to the library yesterday.
        They walked to the library yesterday.

1. Dr. Pasto (paint) his garage last Sunday.
2. Sam (help) him.
3. They (talk) about the weather.
4. We (enjoy) our dinner last night.
5. Mabel (prepare) chicken and fried potatoes.
6. I (look) at some magazines after dinner.
7. Maria (show) us some pictures of Paris last week.
8. She (live) in France for a year.
9. She (like) the women's clothes.

SIMPLE PAST TENSE OF IRREGULAR VERBS

They got up at eight o'clock.
____ took a shower.
____ had breakfast.
____ read the newspaper.
____ went to work.

b   *Make sentences as indicated.*

Example: Peter went to the beach.   (I/to the park)
        I went to the park.

1. You got up at nine o'clock.   (We/at nine thirty)
2. She had a hamburger for lunch.   (Albert/a hot dog)
3. I lost my notebook.   (You/your pen)
4. We saw a movie.   (Our friends/a football game)
5. He took a shower.   (She/a bath)
6. Maria bought a vase.   (I/a chair)
7. You went to the movies.   (We/to the museum)
8. He found a butterfly.   (They/a cat)
9. Mrs. Golo made a chocolate cake.   (I/a sandwich)

c

d

c Sam Brown lives in California. Last month he went to New York and visited his brother Bob. They talked about old times and looked at family photographs. Sam stayed in New York for a week. He enjoyed his visit very much.

1. Where does Sam Brown live?
2. Where did he go last month?
3. Who did he visit there?
4. What did they talk about?
5. What did they look at?
6. How long did Sam stay in New York?
7. Did he enjoy his visit?

d Peter Smith had a good time when he was in Spain. He took his camera with him and got some interesting pictures of Madrid. He thought it was a beautiful city. On his last night there he went to a nice little restaurant called La Cocinita. He had chicken and potatoes for dinner and listened to flamenco music. Before he left Spain, Peter bought some postcards for his friends in Wickam City. Johnnie Wilson met him at the airport when he came home.

1. Did Peter have a good time when he was in Spain?
2. What did he take with him?
3. Did he get pictures of Barcelona or Madrid?
4. What did he think of Madrid?
5. Where did he go on his last night there?
6. What did he have for dinner?
7. Did he listen to flamenco music or rock music?
8. What did Peter buy for his friends before he left Spain?
9. Who met him at the airport when he returned to Wickam City?

AFFIRMATIVE

Peter went to a famous restaurant.
You _____.
They_____.
We _____.
She _____.
I_____.

e *Complete the following sentences using the simple past tense.*

Example: Jimmy and Linda (go) to the art museum.
           Jimmy and Linda went to the art museum.

1. They (take) the bus.
2. They (meet) their friends at the museum.
3. They (see) some beautiful paintings.
4. Jimmy (like) the paintings from England.
5. Linda (enjoy) everything.
6. They (stay) at the museum for an hour.
7. They (eat) lunch at Joe's Snack Bar.
8. Linda (have) a bowl of fruit salad.
9. Jimmy (buy) some candy.

JIMMY: Did you have a good time in
          New York, dad?

SAM: Yes, I did, Jimmy.

JIMMY: What did you and Uncle Bob do?

SAM: We talked about old times.

JIMMY: Did he show you the city?

SAM: Yes, we visited the Statue of
          Liberty and the United Nations.

JIMMY: Did you see any movies?

SAM: No, but we saw a very interesting
          play.

JIMMY: When can we go to New York?

SAM: Next year, Jimmy. You and Linda
          can go with me.

a   *Answer the following questions as indicated.*

Example: What did Sam see in New York? (the Statue of Liberty)
           He saw the Statue of Liberty.

1. Where did Maria go yesterday? (to the movies)
2. Who did she meet at the theater? (Peter)
3. What did he buy her? (some chocolates)
4. What film did they see? (*Spring Song*)
5. Where did they go after the film? (to a coffee shop)
6. Who did they find at the coffee shop? (Barbara and Tino)
7. What did they talk about? (the film)
8. What did they eat? (ice cream)
9. How long did they stay at the coffee shop? (for an hour)

NEGATIVE

Sam didn't see any movies last week.
You _____.
They_____.
We _____.
She _____.
I_____.

b   *Make negative sentences as indicated.*

Example: Sam went to New York. (to Chicago)
           He didn't go to Chicago.

1. He stayed with his brother. (his sister)
2. They talked about old times. (politics)
3. They looked at family photographs. (old magazines)
4. They saw a play. (a movie)
5. Peter went to Spain. (to Italy)
6. He visited Madrid. (Rome)
7. He liked the people. (the weather)
8. He listened to flamenco music. (rock music)
9. He drank wine. (grape juice)

ALBERT: Did you go out Saturday night, Linda?

LINDA: Yes, I went to a party.

ALBERT: What did you do there?

LINDA: We sang and danced all night.

ALBERT: Did they have any food?

LINDA: Yes, they had some delicious
           pastries.

ALBERT: I'm sorry I missed the party.

INTERROGATIVE	SHORT ANSWER FORM	
Did Linda have a good time?	Yes, she did.	No, she didn't.
___ Albert _____ ?	___, he ___.	___, he _____.
___ they _____ ?	___, they___.	___, they____.
___ you _____ ?	___, I ___.	___, I _____.

c *Answer the following questions using the short answer form.*

     Examples: Did Linda stay home Saturday night?
                 No, she didn't.

                 Did she go to a party?
                 Yes, she did.

1. Did she go with Albert?
2. Did she wear jeans?
3. Did she dance at the party?
4. Did they have pastries?
5. Did Sam go to Texas last month?
6. Did he visit his brother?
7. Did they see the Statue of Liberty?
8. Did they go to a movie?
9. Did Sam stay in New York for a month?
10. Did he enjoy his visit?

d *Make questions as indicated.*

     Example: Linda goes out a lot.
               Did she go out last Friday?

1. She sometimes wears a hat.
2. She usually has a good time.
3. Albert often studies at home.
4. He eats a lot of pastries.
5. He sometimes washes the dishes.
6. Barney seldom shaves.
7. He sometimes takes a shower.
8. He usually stops at Nick's Garage.
9. They often play cards.
10. They sometimes go to a movie.

Last Sunday Albert and Jimmy went to the beach. There were hundreds of people there. Jimmy played volleyball and swam in the ocean. But Albert just sat on the beach and watched the girls. It was a hot day and Albert was very thirsty. He wanted a cold drink. Unfortunately, the only restaurant at the beach was closed. The temperature was 90 degrees and Albert was very uncomfortable. Finally he saw a girl with a large picnic basket. It was Jane Garner, a friend from college. Albert carried the basket for her, and she gave him a drink. Five minutes later Jimmy came and sat with them. They ate and drank and had a good time.

a *Answer the following questions about the story.*

   1. Where did Albert and Jimmy go last Sunday?
   2. How many people were there?
   3. What did Jimmy do?
   4. What did Albert do?
   5. What was the weather like?
   6. What did Albert want?
   7. Were there any restaurants open?
   8. Who did Albert see on the beach?
   9. What did she have?
  10. What did she give Albert?
  11. What happened five minutes later?

b *Make questions with **who**, **what**, or **where**.*

   Examples: Albert went <u>to the beach</u>.
              Where did he go?

              He saw <u>Jane Garner</u>.
              Who did he see?

              She gave him <u>a drink</u>.
              What did she give him?

   1. Barney went <u>to the market</u> yesterday.
   2. He bought <u>some apples and pears</u>.
   3. He met <u>Nancy</u> at one o'clock.
   4. She had <u>some old photographs</u>.
   5. They went <u>to the Martinoli Restaurant</u> for lunch.
   6. They ordered <u>chicken and fried potatoes</u>.
   7. They saw <u>Tino</u>.
   8. He talked about <u>Barbara</u>.
   9. She made <u>a cake</u> yesterday.

c *Answer the following questions as indicated.*

   Examples: What did Jane give <u>Albert</u>? (a drink)   What did Sam bring <u>his wife</u>? (some flowers)
              She gave <u>him</u> a drink.   **He brought <u>her</u> some flowers.**

   1. What did Peter buy <u>Maria</u>? (some chocolates)
   2. What did she bring <u>her friends</u>? (a banana cake)
   3. What did they give <u>Otis</u>? (a record player)
   4. What did the students bring <u>Mrs. Golo</u>? (a cat)
   5. What did she give <u>the cat</u>? (some milk)
   6. What did Jack take <u>the Browns</u>? (some old magazines)
   7. What did they give <u>Jack</u>? (an old lamp)
   8. What did Barney show <u>the tourists</u>? (the university)
   9. What did he bring <u>Nancy</u>? (a dog)

d *Change the following sentences to the simple past tense.*

1. Mr. Jones lives in San Francisco.
2. He works at the post office.
3. Every morning he gets up at 7:30 and takes a shower.
4. He usually has coffee and eggs for breakfast.
5. Mr. Jones always goes to work at 8:30.
6. He takes the bus to work.
7. He seldom meets people on the bus.
8. Mr. Jones is a quiet man.
9. He doesn't often talk to strangers.

e *Give short answers to the following questions.*

Example: Linda and Albert are friends, aren't they?
           Yes, they are. OR No, they aren't.

1. Peter drives a sports car, doesn't he?
2.   ıne and Barbara work at the garage, don't they?
3. Barbara doesn't have a boyfriend, does she?
4. Tino is a pilot, isn't he?
5. This book has 300 pages, doesn't it?
6. Sam didn't go to Chicago, did he?
7. He has a brother in New York, doesn't he?
8. They didn't visit the Statue of Liberty, did they?
9. They went to a play, didn't they?

f *Answer the following questions about yourself.*

1. Did you see a movie last week?
2. Where did you go last weekend?
3. How did you go there?
4. What did you do yesterday?
5. Did you see your friends?
6. Did you study last night?
7. What time did you get up this morning?
8. What did you have for breakfast?
9. Did you read the newspaper this morning?
10. What did you do after breakfast?

g   *Look at the pictures and answer the following questions.*

1. Where was Johnnie yesterday?
   He was at home.
2. Where were Anne and Nancy?
   They were at the park.
3. Where was Mrs. Golo?

4. Where was Sam?
5. Where were Maria and Peter?
6. Where was Mr. Bascomb?
7. Where was Jimmy?
8. Where were Barbara and Tino?

h   *Answer the following questions about the pictures.*

1. Was Johnnie at home yesterday?
   Yes, he was.
2. Were Anne and Nancy at the beach?
   No, they weren't. They were at the park.
3. Was Mrs. Golo at the museum?

4. Was Sam at the garage?
5. Were Peter and Maria at the movies?
6. Was Mr. Bascomb at the pet shop?
7. Was Jimmy at the record shop?
8. Were Barbara and Tino at the movies?

i   *Answer the following questions.*

1. What did Johnnie do yesterday?
   He painted the house.
2. What did Anne and Nancy do?
   They played chess.
3. What did Mrs. Golo do?

4. What did Sam do?
5. What did Maria and Peter do?
6. What did Mr. Bascomb do?
7. What did Jimmy do?
8. What did Barbara and Tino do?

j   *Answer the following questions.*

1. Did Johnnie go to the movies yesterday?
   No, he didn't. He painted the house.
2. Did Anne and Nancy play chess?
   Yes, they did.
3. Did Mrs. Golo read a book?

4. Did Sam watch television?
5. Did Maria and Peter go to the opera?
6. Did Mr. Bascomb buy a chair?
7. Did Jimmy listen to records?
8. Did Barbara and Tino play tennis?

k   *Write a short composition about an interesting day. What happened to you? Where were you? Who were you with?*

VOCABULARY

African	degree	finally	later	see	uncomfortable
after	delicious	find		sorry	unfortunately
		flamenco	miss (v.)	start (v.)	
basket	end (v.)		musician	stay	visit (v.)
	enter	hundred			visit (n.)
carry (v.)			pastry	temperature	volleyball
chess	film	key	play (n.)		

EXPRESSIONS

good time   old times   all night   all day

PRONUNCIATION

id

painted	needed	waited
rested	repeated	started
wanted	visited	ended

He painted the house and visited his sister.

The movie started at seven and ended at nine.

She repeated the question and waited for an answer.

d

opened	prepared	rained
closed	loved	stayed
cleaned	showed	called
played	smiled	entered

It rained last Sunday and she stayed home.

She opened the door and he entered.

He showed her the photograph and she smiled.

t

asked	crossed	washed	talked
danced	walked	liked	chased
laughed	worked	looked	watched

Linda laughed and danced all night.

They watched television and talked about football.

Jack walked to the library and looked at magazines.

They worked, rested, and played cards.

She painted the house, washed the car, and cleaned the kitchen.

He liked, loved, and needed his dog.

SIMPLE PAST Affirmative

He She I You We They	walked drove took the bus	to class last week.

Negative

He She I You We They	didn't (did not)	walk drive take the bus	last week.

Interrogative

Did	he she I you we they	walk drive take the bus	last week?

Short Answers

Yes,	he she I you we they	did.

No,	he she I you we they	didn't.

SIMPLE PAST Irregular Verbs

He	bought ate took found had	some candy yesterday.

Regular Verbs

They	danced talked	at the party.
	worked lived	in New York.

Question with WHERE, WHEN, WHO, WHAT

Anne went to the park.	Where did she go?	To the park.
She left at 12 o'clock.	When did she leave?	12 o'clock.
She met Nancy.	Who did she meet?	Nancy.
They played chess.	What did they play?	Chess.

CHAPTER THIRTEEN

Future with "going to"   **Adverbs of manner**

a

b

c

d

a   Peter is packing his suitcase. He's preparing for another trip. Tomorrow he's going to travel to France. He's going to stay in Paris for a week. He's going to visit the Eiffel Tower.

1. What's Peter doing?
2. What's he going to do tomorrow?
3. How long is he going to stay in Paris?
4. What's he going to do there?

b   Albert is picking up the phone. He's going to call Linda. He's going to invite her to a movie. He's going to drive his father's car.

1. What's Albert doing?
2. Who's he going to call?
3. Is he going to invite her to a movie or a concert?
4. Is he going to take a taxi or drive his father's car?

c   Mrs. Brown went to the market this morning. She bought some chocolate, eggs, flour, and sugar. She's going to make a chocolate cake for Jimmy. It's his birthday tomorrow. He's going to have a party.

1. Where did Mrs. Brown go this morning?
2. What did she buy?
3. What's she going to make?
4. When's Jimmy going to have his party?

d   Tino is at the florist's. He's looking at some flowers. He's going to buy some carnations. He's going to give them to Barbara.

1. Where's Tino?
2. What's he looking at?
3. What's he going to buy?
4. Who's he going to give them to?

AFFIRMATIVE

Peter's going to stay in Paris.
He's _____.
Mary's _____.
She's _____.

We're going to visit London.
They're_____.
You're _____.
I'm _____.

e   *Answer the following questions about the stories above.*

Example: Is Peter going to travel to England?
            No, he's going to travel to France.

1. Is he going to stay in Paris for a month?
2. Is he going to visit the Tower of London?
3. Is Albert going to call Jane?
4. Is he going to invite her to a concert?
5. Is he going to drive his mother's car?
6. Is Mrs. Brown going to make an orange cake?
7. Is Jimmy going to have his birthday party next week?
8. Is Tino going to buy some roses?
9. Is he going to give them to Maria?

MABEL BROWN: What are you going to do this weekend?

SAM BROWN: I'm going to plant some banana trees.

MABEL BROWN: Where are you going to plant them?

SAM BROWN: In back of the house.

MABEL BROWN: What are you going to do then?

SAM BROWN: I'm going to sit down and relax.

JIMMY: What are you going to do tonight?

LINDA: I'm going to see a movie with Albert.

JIMMY: With Albert? But he doesn't have a car.

LINDA: He's going to drive his father's car.

INTERROGATIVE

Is Linda going to stay home?
_ she _____ ?
_ Albert _____ ?
_ he _____ ?

Are they going to play tennis?
____ you _____ ?
____ we _____ ?
____ the Browns _____ ?

f   *Make questions with **going to**.*

Example: Sam is going to stay home.   (watch television)
       Is he going to watch television?

1. He's going to work in the back yard.   (plant apple trees)
2. Albert and Linda are going to see a movie.   (take the bus)
3. They're going to have dinner after the movie.   (eat at home)
4. Peter is preparing for another trip.   (visit Germany)
5. He's packing his suitcase.   (take his camera)
6. He's going to visit France.   (stay in Nice)
7. Tino is going to see Barbara tonight.   (give her some flowers)
8. They're going to have a party next week.   (invite Peter and Maria)
9. Maria is working at the hospital today.   (have lunch there)

NEGATIVE

Linda isn't going to stay home.
She _____ .
Albert _____ .
He _____ .

They aren't going to play tennis.
You _____ .
We _____ .
The Browns _____ .

g   *Make negative sentences with **going to**.*

Example: Sam is going to work in the back yard.   (in the house)
       He isn't going to work in the house.

1. He's going to plant banana trees.   (apple trees)
2. Albert and Linda are going to see a movie.   (a play)
3. They're going to take the car.   (the bus)
4. They're going to have dinner after the movie.   (before the movie)
5. They're going to eat in a Mexican restaurant.   (at home)
6. Peter is going to visit France.   (Germany)
7. He's going to stay in Paris.   (in Nice)
8. Tino is going to see Barbara tonight.   (Maria)
9. They're going to play chess.   (cards)

a   Barbara is a good secretary. She types quickly and accurately. She listens carefully and doesn't make mistakes. Barbara works very well.

1. What kind of secretary is Barbara?
2. How does she type?
3. Does she listen carefully?
4. Does she make mistakes?
5. How does she work?

b   Anne is a bad secretary. She types slowly and makes a lot of mistakes. She doesn't listen carefully and works badly.

1. What kind of secretary is Anne?
2. How does she type?
3. Does she make mistakes?
4. Does she listen carefully?
5. How does she work?

ADVERBS OF MANNER

She's a good typist.   She types well.
_____ bad _____ .   _____ badly.
_____ slow _____ .   _____ slowly.
_____ quick _____ .   _____ quickly.
_____ careful _____ .   _____ carefully.

c   *Change the following sentences, using adverbs.*

Examples: Anne is a slow worker. _*She works slowly.*_

Dr. Pasto is a good speaker. _*He speaks well.*_

1. Jack is a good cook. _____

2. He's a dangerous driver. _____

3. Fred is a careful writer. _____

4. He's a slow reader. _____

5. Mrs. Golo is a bad dancer. _____

6. She's a good singer. _____

7. Barbara is a quick typist. _____

8. She's a careful driver. _____

MR. BASCOMB: You're working slowly, Miss Jones.

ANNE JONES: That's because I'm working carefully.

MR. BASCOMB: But you make a lot of mistakes.

ANNE JONES: I know, Mr. Bascomb.

MR. BASCOMB: Perhaps I don't speak clearly.

ANNE JONES: No, I understand you perfectly.

MR. BASCOMB: Then what's the problem?

ANNE JONES: I don't know, Mr. Bascomb.

1

2

3

4

5

6

7

8

d *Look at the pictures and make a sentence about each one using an adverb.*

1. (loud) Mrs. Golo _____ *speaks loudly* . _____

2. (soft) Barbara _____

3. (dangerous) Jack _____

4. (careful) Barney _____

5. (good) Otis and Gloria _____

6. (beautiful) Anne _____

7. (quick) Albert _____

8. (slow) Fred _____

e *Answer the following questions about the pictures as indicated.*

1. Does Mrs. Golo speak loudly?
   Yes, she does.
2. Does Barbara speak loudly?
   No, she doesn't. She speaks softly.
3. Does Jack drive carefully?

4. Does Barney drive carefully?
5. Do Otis and Gloria dance badly?
6. Does Anne sing beautifully?
7. Does Albert eat quickly?
8. Does Fred read quickly?

f *Make questions with* **how.**

Example: Barney drives carefully. (Nancy)
          How does Nancy drive?

1. Anne sings beautifully. (Barbara)
2. Linda writes well. (Jimmy)
3. Fred dresses badly. (Barney)
4. Barbara speaks softly. (Mrs. Golo)
5. Jack drives dangerously. (Peter)

6. Mabel cooks well. (Nancy)
7. Albert types slowly. (Jimmy)
8. Gloria and Otis dance well.
   (Peter and Maria)
9. Barbara works quickly. (Anne)

g *Describe how you do the following activities, using the adverbs* **quickly, slowly, carefully, well,**
badly, loudly, softly, *and* **beautifully.**

Examples: sing   walk
          I sing well.   **I walk quickly.**

1. dance
2. play chess
3. read
4. walk
5. eat

6. write
7. speak
8. dress
9. work
10. sing

There's a big crowd of people at the Odeon Theater tonight. They're waiting
anxiously for Ula Hackey, the famous Hollywood actress. She's going to
attend the première of her new film, *Sweet Summer.* Everyone is very excited.
Miss Hackey is coming now. She's waving happily to the crowd. The man
next to her is a television announcer. He's going to ask Miss Hackey some
questions about her new film. There are some photographers following the
actress. They're going to take pictures of her for the newspapers.
She's a very popular star. After the film, Miss Hackey is going to sign
autographs and talk to the people.

a *Answer the following questions about the story.*

1. Who are the people waiting for?
2. Why is she at the Odeon Theater tonight?
3. Who is she waving to?
4. Who is the man next to Miss Hackey?
5. What's he going to do?

6. Who are the men following the actress?
7. What are they going to do?
8. Why do they want pictures of Miss Hackey?
9. What is she going to do after the film?

b *Make questions with **going to**.*

Example: Maria/take a bath
Is Maria going to take a bath?

1. she/wash her hair
2. she/meet Peter tonight
3. they/see a play
4. Peter/drive his car
5. he/come at eight o'clock

6. he/bring some flowers
7. Maria/wear a red dress
8. she/take a coat
9. they/eat at the Martinoli Restaurant

c *Make negative sentences with **going to**, as indicated.*

Examples: I/wear a hat
I'm not going to wear a hat.

She/take her umbrella.
She isn't going to take her umbrella.

1. He/come to the party
2. They/watch television
3. She/study in the library
4. You/take the bus
5. I/write a letter

6. She/live in New York
7. We/visit the museum
8. They/go to the park
9. He/play baseball

d *Answer the following questions about yourself.*

Example: What are you going to do after class?
I'm going to meet some friends/see a movie/etc.

1. Is it going to rain today?
2. Are you going to walk home?
3. What are you going to do tonight?
4. Who are you going to see?
5. What are you going to have for dinner?

6. What are you going to do tomorrow?
7. What time are you going to get up?
8. Are you going to see your friends tomorrow?
9. What are you going to do this weekend?

e *Write a short composition about what you are going to do next weekend.*

VOCABULARY

accurately	carnation	invite	quick	suitcase
actress	clearly		quickly	
announcer	concert	loud		then
anxiously	crowd		reader	tomorrow
attend		mistake	relax	typist
autograph	excite			
		pack (v.)	sign (v.)	worker
back	florist	perfectly	slow	writer
badly	flour	phone	slowly	
	follow	photographer	soft	
careful		popular	speaker	
carefully	happily	première	star	

EXPRESSIONS

for a week

for a month

Future Time Expressions

tonight	this weekend
tomorrow	next week
tomorrow morning	next month
tomorrow night	next year

PRONUNCIATION

	e			**ey**	
hotel	left	President	grade	radiator	favorite
weekend	pet	September	shape	education	dangerous
forget	attend	seldom	late	conversation	game
chess	when	expression	table	mistake	sale

The President went to Mexico in September.
Fred seldom gets dressed before seven.

Take the vase from the table.
Jane made a cake for David.

The famous chess player seldom made a mistake.
She never lost a game of chess.

GOING TO   Affirmative

He She	's (is)		see a movie.
I	'm (am)	going to	play tennis.
You We They	're (are)		visit Paris.

Negative

He She	isn't 's not (is not)		see a movie.
I	'm not (am not)	going to	play tennis.
You We They	aren't 're not (are not)		visit Paris.

Interrogative

Is	he she		see a movie?
Am	I	going to	play tennis?
Are	you we they		visit Paris?

Short Answers

	he she	is.
Yes,	I	am.
	you we they	are.

	he she	isn't.
No,	I	'm not.
	you we they	aren't.

He's going to	work in London. leave next month. write to his wife. buy a suitcase.

Question with WHERE, WHEN, WHO, WHAT

Where's he going to work? When's he going to leave? Who's he going to write to? What's he going to buy?	In London. Next month. His wife. A suitcase.

Question with HOW

How does she	work? drive?

ADVERBS OF MANNER

She	works drives	well. badly. slowly. quickly. carefully.

CHAPTER FOURTEEN

Review

NANCY'S JOURNEY

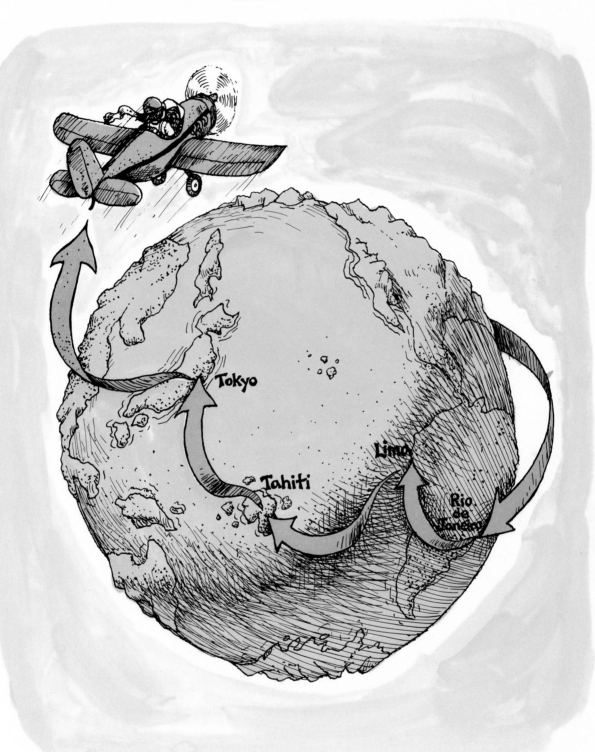

Last summer Nancy Paine flew around the world. She started in New York and made her first stop in Rio de Janeiro. Rio is a wonderful city and Nancy made some good friends there. They taught her a few words of Portuguese and she learned the samba.

After a week in Rio, Nancy continued her journey. She flew over some very high mountains called the Andes and landed in Lima, Peru. She walked around the capital and took photographs of the beautiful old churches. Nancy left Peru on a fine, sunny day. She traveled across the Pacific Ocean to the island of Tahiti.

It was a very long trip, more than two thousand miles. But the weather was good, and she didn't have any problems. Nancy loved the people of Tahiti, and she had a good time there. She sailed a small boat and swam in the ocean every day. The sun was always hot and the beaches were beautiful. Everything was perfect.

After two weeks Nancy got back in her plane and left for Japan. She stayed in Tokyo for a couple of days, in a small hotel near the center of the city. She found a very nice teahouse across the street from her hotel. Nancy enjoyed the lovely gardens there. She also admired the traditional clothes of the Japanese women.

Nancy's next stop was Moscow, Russia. She had some rough weather on the way. But Nancy is an expert pilot, and she arrived at her destination without any serious trouble. In Moscow she bought a fur coat and saw some folk dancers.

The last stop on Nancy's journey was Paris, the "City of Light." She visited some friends in the Latin Quarter, and they took her to a fine restaurant near the river Seine. Nancy ate frog legs and drank some delicious white wine. Her friends asked a lot of questions about her travels, and she told them everything. It was quite a journey.

a   *Answer the following questions about Nancy's journey.*

1. What did Nancy Paine do last summer?
2. Where did she start?
3. Where did she make her first stop?
4. What did Nancy learn in Rio?
5. Where did she go after Brazil?
6. What did she do in Lima?
7. What was Nancy's next stop?
8. What did she do in Tahiti?
9. Did she have a good time there?
10. Where did Nancy go after Tahiti?
11. How long did she stay in Tokyo?
12. What did she find across the street from her hotel?
13. What did Nancy admire about the Japanese women?
14. What was her next stop?
15. What did she buy there?
16. What did she see?
17. Where did Nancy go after Moscow?
18. Who did she visit there?
19. Where did they take her?
20. What did she drink?

b   *Complete the following sentences using* **there's a, there's some,** *or* **there are some.**

Examples: _There are some_ _____ glasses on the shelf.

   There's some _____ ice cream in the kitchen.

1. _____ roses in the garden.

2. _____ bread on the table.

3. _____ photographs in the desk.

4. _____ football in the closet.

5. _____ soup in the kitchen.

6. _____ clock in the living room.

7. _____ dishes in the sink.

8. _____ sugar next to the coffeepot.

9. _____ vase by the window.

10. _____ tomato juice in the can.

c   *Change the sentences as indicated.*

Examples: Peter needs some matches.
           He doesn't have any.

           They need a car.
           They don't have one.

1. She needs some toothpaste.
2. I need some shampoo.
3. Jack needs a raincoat.
4. He needs some money.
5. We need a dictionary.
6. They need some butter.
7. Maria needs a teapot.
8. She needs some sugar.
9. Wickam City needs a good hotel.

d   *Answer the following questions as indicated.*

Example: Does Anne listen to the radio? (No/seldom)
           No, she seldom listens to the radio.

1. Does she play the guitar? (Yes/often)
2. Does Barney stop at Nick's Garage? (Yes/always)
3. Do they talk about politics? (No/seldom)
4. Do they play cards? (Yes/sometimes)
5. Does Mrs. Golo feed the cat? (Yes/always)
6. Does she cut the grass? (No/never)
7. Do Mr. and Mrs. Bascomb go to the theater? (Yes/often)
8. Do they take the bus? (No/never)
9. Does Mr. Bascomb smoke cigars? (Yes/usually)

e   *Make questions as indicated.*

Example: Maria takes a bath every day.
          Is she taking a bath now?

1. Jimmy often studies with his friends.
2. He usually helps them with their lessons.
3. They walk home from school every day.
4. Mr. and Mrs. Bascomb often play chess.
5. She usually wins.
6. He seldom talks to her after a game.
7. Mr. Grubb goes to the park every afternoon.
8. Sometimes he reads the newspaper.
9. He usually feeds the pigeons.

f   *Look at the pictures of Peter and make sentences about what he is doing now.*

1. **He's getting up.**

g   *Make sentences about what he does every day.*

1. **He gets up.**

h   *Make sentences about what he did yesterday.*

1. **He got up.**

i   *Answer the following questions about yourself, using the short answer form.*

Examples: Do you often get up before eight o'clock?
Yes, I do. OR **No, I don't.**

Did you get up before eight o'clock this morning?
Yes, I did. OR **No, I didn't.**

1. Do you often make breakfast?
2. Did you make breakfast this morning?
3. Do you usually take the bus?
4. Did you take the bus yesterday?
5. Did you go to the library yesterday?
6. Did you go to the park?
7. Do you often listen to records?
8. Did you listen to records yesterday?
9. Did you watch television?

j   *Make questions as indicated.*

Example: Maria took the bus yesterday.
Does she often take the bus?

1. She went to the museum.
2. She had a good time.
3. Barbara and Tino played tennis yesterday.
4. She won.
5. They listened to the radio.
6. Albert got up at seven o'clock this morning.
7. He had orange juice and eggs for breakfast.
8. The Browns worked in the garden last Sunday.
9. Sam cut the grass.

k *Complete the following sentences using the simple past tense.*

Example: Tino ____*went*____ to the florist's and ____*bought*____ some flowers.   (go/buy)

1. Barney _____ all day yesterday.   (work)

2. He _____ a lot of tourists at the airport.   (meet)

3. He _____ them to the Wickam Hotel.   (take)

4. After work he _____ to Nick's Garage.   (go)

5. His friends _____ all there.   (be)

6. They _____ Coke and _____ cards.   (drink/play)

7. Barney _____ every game. He never _____.   (win/lose)

8. He _____ a good time with his friends.   (have)

9. Barney _____ the garage at eight-thirty.   (leave)

10. He _____ in his taxi and _____ home.   (get/drive)

Daisy Humple has a small apartment near the center of Wickam City. Her boyfriend, Simon, is a magician. He lives a long way from Daisy, on the other side of town. Every weekend he appears at her apartment. He usually brings her chocolates or flowers. He pulls them out of his hat. Sometimes Daisy and Simon play cards. He always wins, and Daisy thinks he is lucky. Actually, Simon never loses at cards or any other game. He is very clever, and he is also very amusing. He tells a lot of funny stories, and she always laughs. Simon and Daisy are very happy together. But they're a mysterious couple. They often disappear on weekends, and nobody knows where they go.

l *Answer the following questions about the story.*

1. Where is Daisy's apartment?
2. What is her boyfriend's name?
3. Does he live near Daisy?
4. When does he come to her apartment?
5. What does he usually bring her?
6. Who always wins when Simon and Daisy play cards?
7. Why does Daisy always laugh when she is with Simon?
8. Why are Simon and Daisy a mysterious couple?

m *Change the story about Simon and Daisy to the simple past tense.*

n   *Complete the following sentences as indicated.*

Example: Simon is going to Daisy's. He's taking ___*his*___ cards with ___*him*___ .

1. Linda is going to class. She's taking _____ notebook with _____ .

2. They're going to the park. They're taking _____ lunch with _____ .

3. Peter is going to the movies. He's taking _____ girlfriend with _____ .

4. I'm going to work. I'm taking _____ umbrella with _____ .

5. She's going to the market. She's taking _____ shopping bag with _____ .

6. We're going to the beach. We're taking _____ friends with _____ .

7. He's going to Mexico. He's taking _____ camera with _____ .

8. They're going to New York. They're taking _____ children with _____ .

9. Anne is going to the party. She's taking _____ guitar with _____ .

o   *Complete each of the following sentences using a possessive adjective and a possessive pronoun.*

Example: Nancy brought ___*her*___ dictionary and I brought ___*mine*___ .

1. They washed _____ clothes and we washed _____ .

2. You drove _____ car and he drove _____ .

3. Albert took _____ coat and Linda took _____ .

4. I forgot _____ umbrella and they forgot _____ .

5. You painted _____ house and we painted _____ .

6. He visited _____ family and I visited _____ .

7. We wrote to _____ friends and they wrote to _____ .

8. She found _____ pen and you found _____ .

9. He took _____ camera and we took _____ .

p   *Answer the following questions about yourself.*

1. How many books did you read last month?
2. How many letters did you write last week?
3. Did you go to a movie last Saturday?
4. What time did you have lunch yesterday?
5. Where did you eat?
6. What did you have for lunch?
7. What time did you get up this morning?
8. What time did you leave the house?
9. Did you take the bus?
10. What time did this class start?

1

2

3

4

5

6

7

8

q *Look at the pictures and answer the following questions.*

1. What's Peter going to do?
   He's going to wash the car.
2. What are Mr. and Mrs. Bascomb going to do?
3. What's Jack going to do?
4. What's Anne going to do?
5. What are Jimmy and his friends going to do?
6. What's Barney going to do?
7. What's Tino going to do?
8. What are Otis and Gloria going to do?

r *Answer the following questions as indicated.*

1. Is Peter going to wash the dishes?
   No, he isn't. He's going to wash the car.
2. Are Mr. and Mrs. Bascomb going to eat dinner?
   Yes, they are.
3. Is Jack going to shave?
4. Is Anne going to call the fire department?
5. Are Jimmy and his friends going to play tennis?
6. Is Barney going to take a bath?
7. Is Tino going to buy some candy?
8. Are Otis and Gloria going to play cards?

s *Answer the following questions, using opposites.*

Example: Does Albert eat slowly?
          No, he eats quickly.

1. Does Jack drive carefully?
2. Does Anne work well?
3. Does Mrs. Golo speak softly?
4. Does Fred read quickly?
5. Does Barbara work badly?
6. Does she speak loudly?
7. Does Albert run quickly?
8. Does Otis dance badly?
9. Does Barney drive dangerously?

t *Give short answers to the following questions.*

Example: You like rock music, don't you?
          Yes, I do. OR **No, I don't.**

1. You don't have a record player, do you?
2. You're going out tonight, aren't you?
3. You aren't going to a movie, are you?
4. You got up at eight o'clock this morning, didn't you?
5. You didn't have eggs for breakfast, did you?
6. You had a good time last night, didn't you?
7. You weren't at home, were you?
8. You dance very well, don't you?
9. You don't play tennis, do you?

u   *Complete the following sentences using suitable prepositions.*

Example: They're taking pictures ___*of*___ Miss Hackey ___*for*___ the newspapers.

1. Peter is driving _____ Los Angeles _____ San Francisco.

2. He's taking his dog _____ him.

3. Tino is taking orders _____ the Hambys.

4. Mrs. Hamby wants a bowl _____ vegetable soup _____ dinner.

5. Tino doesn't have any pictures _____ Italy _____ the wall.

6. Last summer Nancy traveled _____ the world.

7. She flew _____ some high mountains _____ South America.

8. She traveled _____ the Pacific Ocean _____ the island of Tahiti.

9. She stayed _____ Tahiti _____ a couple _____ weeks.

VOCABULARY

admire	disappear	magician	plane	teahouse
appear		mile	problem	teapot
	frog legs	mountain	pull (v.)	than
boat	funny	mysterious		thousand
			quite	together
candy	journey	nobody		
church			raincoat	world
clever	land (v.)	ocean		
continue	learn		sail (v.)	
couple	lovely	perfect	shopping bag	

TEST

1. He is _____.

   a. one artist   c. an artist
   b. a artist   d. artist

2. _____ does she go to work?
   At nine o'clock.

   a. Why   c. When
   b. Where   d. How

3. _____ does she take the bus?
   Because she doesn't have a car.

   a. Why   c. When
   b. Where   d. How

4. He takes good care _____ his
   motorcycle.

   a. for   c. to
   b. of   d. with

5. They need some gas. They're
   looking _____ a gas station.

   a. for   c. from
   b. to   d. at

6. There aren't any pictures
   _____ the wall.

   a. to   c. in
   b. at   d. on

7. Nancy traveled _____ the world.

   a. over   c. across
   b. on   d. around

8. She flew _____ high mountains.

   a. over   c. in
   b. under   d. at

9. She was _____ Paris last month.

   a. to   c. in
   b. at   d. from

10. There's a park across the
    street _____ the hospital.

    a. of   c. to
    b. from   d. for

11. They asked a lot of questions
    _____ his job.

    a. about   c. for
    b. of   d. on

12. Is this typewriter _____?

    a. your   c. to you
    b. yours   d. you

13. The boys are washing _____ clothes.

    a. there   c. theirs
    b. their   d. they're

14. Whose car is that? It's _____.

    a. to her   c. hers
    b. her   d. Mrs. Jacobs

15. He's taking _____ some chocolates.

    a. her   c. hers
    b. to her   d. she

16. She's telling _____ an amusing
    story.

    a. they   c. to them
    b. them   d. their

17. Don't talk _____.

    a. him   c. to him
    b. he   d. at him

18. _____ coffee in the pot.

    a. It's a   c. There's a
    b. It has   d. There's some

19. _____ magazines in the closet.

    a. They're   c. There
    b. Their   d. There are

20. _____ bottle in the sink.

    a. It has a   c. There's a
    b. It's a   d. There are

21. She _____ the bus every day.

    a. taking   c. takes
    b. is taking   d. take

22. They _____ football now.

    a. is playing   c. play
    b. plays   d. are playing

23. I never _____ coffee.

    a. drink   c. drinking
    b. am drinking d. to drink

24. He _____ today.

    a. are working c. work
    b. is working   d. working

25. Does Anne like music? Yes,
    she _____.

    a. do   c. does
    b. likes   d. does like

26. Do they always watch television?
    Yes, they _____.

    a. watch   c. do watch
    b. do   d. does

27. We often _____ dinner at six.

    a. having   c. are having
    b. has   d. have

28. Linda is thirsty. She wants
    _____ glass of milk.

    a. other   c. any
    b. some   d. another

29. The _____ lamp is in the bedroom.

    a. other   c. another
    b. any   d. other one

30. I don't need _____ money.

    a. some   c. another
    b. any   d. a

31. They have _____ butter.

    a. some   c. a
    b. any   d. one

32. Albert has a good radio.
    He doesn't need _____.

    a. other one   c. some
    b. any   d. another one

33. She doesn't have any sugar. She
    needs _____.

    a. any   c. some
    b. one   d. another

34. They _____ in New York last week.

    a. are   c. was
    b. were   d. went

35. Maria _____ at home yesterday.

    a. is   c. was
    b. were   d. went

36. Did she _____ that movie?

    a. saw   c. see
    b. seeing d. look

37. Peter didn't _____ dinner.

    a. prepare   c. preparing
    b. prepared   d. prepares

38. They _____ at the Martinoli
    Restaurant last night.

    a. eat   c. eating
    b. did eat d. ate

39. Did Anne wash the dishes? Yes,
    she _____.

    a. did   c. is washing
    b. did wash d. washed

40. Did they have dinner at home?
    No, they _____.

    a. didn't have   c. have not
    b. didn't   d. don't

IRREGULAR VERBS

INFINITIVE	PAST TENSE	INFINITIVE	PAST TENSE	INFINITIVE	PAST TENSE
be	was/were	give	gave	sing	sang
bring	brought	go	went	sit	sat
buy	bought	have	had	speak	spoke
come	came	hold	held	stand	stood
cut	cut	know	knew	swim	swam
do	did	leave	left	take	took
drink	drank	lose	lost	teach	taught
drive	drove	make	made	tell	told
eat	ate	meet	met	think	thought
feed	fed	put	put	understand	understood
find	found	read	read	wear	wore
fly	flew	ride	rode	win	won
forget	forgot	see	saw	write	wrote
get	got	shine	shone		

VOCABULARY

This vocabulary includes all the words used in the text, along with the number of the page on which the word appears for the first time. Nouns are given in the singular only. Verbs are given here in the infinitive form; to find the past tense of irregular verbs, see page 223.

Parts of speech have been omitted except for words that can be used as more than one part of speech. These abbreviations are used: adj. = adjective; adv. = adverb; n. = noun; prep. = preposition; v. = verb.

a, 3
about, 60
accurately, 200
across, 48
actress, 204
address (n.), 48
admire, 211
African, 179
after, 180
afternoon, 47
ah, 42
air, 141
airplane, 14
airport, 10
all, 49
alone, 173
already, 149
also, 82
always, 118
am, 2
American, 18
amusing, 141
an, 4
and, 2
animal, 154
announcer, 204
another, 137
answer, 43
antique shop, 66
anxiously, 204
any, 89
anyone, 167
apartment, 76
appear, 216
appetite, 152
apple, 7
April, 169
are, 2
around, 90
art, 106

artist, 4
ask, 43
at, 10
athlete, 152
attend, 204
August, 112
autograph, 204
away, 49

back (n.), 197
bad, 21
badly, 200
ball, 9
ballet, 21
banana, 118
bank, 10
banker, 3
baseball, 152
basket, 187
basketball, 66
bath, 56
bathroom, 66
bathtub, 98
beach, 68
beautiful, 17
because, 141
bed, 98
bedroom, 98
beer, 174
before, 118
behind, 9
belong, 98
bench, 125
bicycle, 22
big, 31
bill, 64
bird, 7
birthday, 106
black, 29
blackboard, 36

blond, 21
boat, 210
bone, 127
book, 6
bookcase, 9
boot, 90
bottle, 6
bowl, 91
box, 91
boy, 22
boyfriend, 84
brand-new, 24
Brazilian, 27
bread, 91
bread crumb, 125
breakfast, 64
bring, 40
brother, 67
brown, 74
brush (v.), 56
building, 28
bus, 12
business, 20
businessman, 3
bus stop, 12
but, 73
butter, 91
butterfly, 97
buy, 66
by, 88

cafe, 88
cake, 94
calendar, 170
call (v.), 40
camera, 72
can (n.), 91
can (v.), 154
candle, 40
candy, 219

capital, 27
car, 11
card, 8
care (n.), 141
careful, 200
carefully, 200
carnation, 196
carry, 187
cashier, 59
cat, 7
center, 141
cereal, 91
certainly, 107
chair, 6
chase (v.), 97
cheap, 22
cheese, 91
cherry, 92
chess, 178
chicken, 7
chocolate, 94
church, 210
cigar, 66
cigarette, 141
city, 27
class, 37
classical, 100
classroom, 28
clean (adj.), 22
clearly, 201
clever, 216
clock, 6
close (v.), 36
closet, 137
clothes, 148
cloudy, 164
coat, 6
Coca-Cola, 43
coffee, 50
coffeepot, 92

coffee shop, 58
Coke, 58
cold, 17
collection, 97
college, 125
color, 24
come, 38
company, 141
composition, 107
concert, 196
construction, 173
continue, 210
conversation, 141
cook (n.), 154
cookie, 92
corner, 11
counter, 62
country, 21
country singer, 21
couple, 216
cowboy, 20
cross (v.), 111
crowd, 204
cup, 41
customer, 134
cut (v.), 63

damp, 164
dance (v.), 39
dancer, 21
dangerous, 49
darts, 59
daughter, 83
day, 45
December, 106
degree, 187
delicious, 185
department, 48
desk, 28
dessert, 155

soft, 203
some, 88
sometimes, 121
son, 83
song, 152
sonny, 149
sorry, 185
soup, 91
spaghetti, 94
speak, 119
speaker, 200
sport, 100
sports car, 120
spring (n.), 168
stamp (n.), 73
stand (v.), 36
star (n.), 204
start (v.), 178
statue, 97
stay, 186
step (n.), 90
stop (v.), 141
store, 111
storekeeper, 140
story, 141
stove, 98
strange, 106
street, 48
strong, 106
student, 19
study (v.), 112
stupid, 31
subject, 125
sugar, 139
suitcase, 196
summer, 168
sun, 65
Sunday, 65
sunny, 164
swim (v.), 157

table, 6
take, 40

talk, 37
talker, 107
tall, 21
tango, 154
tank, 148
taxi, 72
taxi driver, 11
tea, 56
teacher, 28
teahouse, 211
teapot, 213
teeth, 56
telegram, 67
telephone, 43
television, 60
tell, 135
temperature, 187
ten, 25
tennis, 134
tenth, 169
terrible, 164
than, 210
thank you, 2
that, 5
the, 10
theater, 88
their, 78
them, 38
then, 197
there, 38
these, 8
they, 8
thin, 22
thing, 71
think, 65
third, 169
thirsty, 17
thirteen, 25
thirteenth, 169
thirtieth, 169
thirty, 44
this, 3
those, 8

thousand, 210
three, 25
Thursday, 169
tie (n.), 138
time, 26
tire (v.), 141
to, 2
today, 63
together, 216
toilet, 98
tomato, 94
tomorrow, 196
tonight, 39
too, 5
toothpaste, 150
tourist, 18
towel, 148
town, 141
toy, 173
traditional, 97
trash, 90
travel, 164
tree, 11
trip, 165
truck, 12
true, 107
truth, 167
Tuesday, 169
TV, 74
twelfth, 169
twelve, 25
twentieth, 169
twenty, 25
two, 25
type (v.), 156
typewriter, 74
typist, 200

ugly, 31
umbrella, 29
uncle, 78
uncomfortable, 187
under, 9

understand, 119
unfortunately, 187
unhappy, 164
university, 28
unusual, 106
up, 36
us, 38
use (v.), 155
useful, 141
usually, 121

vacation, 164
vase, 9
vegetable, 82
vegetarian, 106
very, 21
violin, 154
visit (n.), 182
visit (v.), 182
visitor, 97
volleyball, 187

wait (v.), 49
waiter, 2
waitress, 93
walk (v.), 62
wall, 41
wallet, 75
want, 93
warm, 164
was, 164
wash (v.), 50
wash basin, 98
wastebasket, 30
watch (n.), 6
watch (v.), 99
water, 67
way, 118
we, 19
wear, 56
weather, 120
Wednesday, 155
week, 66

weekend, 164
weight, 155
well (adv.), 141
were, 164
wet, 148
what, 2
when, 108
where, 12
white, 83
who, 5
whose, 79
why, 98
wide, 97
wife, 57
win (v.), 135
window, 27
windy, 164
wine, 94
winter, 168
wire (n.), 90
with, 38
woman, 22
wonderful, 71
word, 119
work (n.), 28
worker, 200
world, 210
worry, 49
write, 36
writer, 200

yard, 90
year, 45
yellow, 99
yes, 6
yesterday, 164
you, 2
young, 22
yours, 2